Best Prescriptions
To Better You

Best Prescriptions
To Better You

by
Dr. Herminio L. Gamponia, MD, FACIP

Order this book online at www.trafford.com
or email orders@trafford.com

Most Trafford titles are also available at major online book retailers.

© Copyright 2012 Dr. Herminio L. Gamponia, MD, FACIP.

Print information available on the last page.

ISBN: 978-1-4669-0379-1 (sc)
ISBN: 978-1-4669-0380-7 (e)

Trafford rev. 01/22/2021

 www.trafford.com

North America & international
toll-free: 844-688-6899 (USA & Canada)
fax: 812 355 4082

Acknowledgements

I am most grateful to the following wonderful friends:

Mrs. Judy Greenleaf, a retired school teacher in the Roane County Public School System. She helped with some corrections on my commas, semicolons, and some wording.

Mrs. Cindy Heilman, dedicated wife of Pastor Joe Heilman at the Methodist Memorial Church in Spencer, who prepares the worship service programs, including the Bible classes that I enjoy because of the many questions she asks. She corrected most of my tenses.

My daughter, Julie Gamponia, who is currently working as a missionary in Thailand. She did a wonderful job editing most of my articles.

Mrs. Brenda Knapp, Executive Assistant to the CEO at Roane General Hospital, who retyped and formatted this book. The final format of the manuscript would not have been possible without her generous contribution.

Lastly, my wife, Phoebe Gamponia, who has been most patient with me while I took the time to write this manuscript.

Table of Contents

Introduction

I entitled this book *"Best Prescriptions To Better You"* because it gives advice on how to wisely use our time on earth. I view it as a sort of prescription for life, and as a physician-surgeon who has written numerous prescriptions each day for over thirty years, I feel I have something good to share. This book is unique in format because, while some of the articles are essays, others tend to outline instructions with explanations. This book is simple and clear, yet, the lessons are important to learn and follow. It gives specific examples on how to apply these important principles in our daily activities. This book is a collection of my writings over the past ten years.

My faith in God is unbreakable. Because of the many incredible interactions and support with which He has blessed me, I have chosen to have the Ten Commandments as the first article.

There was a time when I mentally asked many questions about life. There was someone in my thoughts to answer every question. When I was at Harvard taking a review course in general surgery, I asked many questions, and the answers would also come from the Bible. I would open the Bible at random and wherever I focused my eyes, there were the verses that answered my questions.

I thought that I had lost my personal contact with God, but when I asked a question about why the numerous planets did not bump against one another, the answer came to my thoughts saying, "Why don't you visit the Boston Museum of Science nearby. You can get many explanations there." Until then, I didn't even know that there was a museum nearby. I spent many afternoons there, learning things about science, such as how radio broadcasts are transferred from one station to another, or how TV works with audio and visual images. The museum provided a review of the Cooper's Law, Newton's Law, the speed of light, and the work of Albert Einstein. I even saw chickens hatched every thirty minutes, and many other physical laws were also demonstrated.

I bought three books: The Laws of Success by Napoleon Hill, Success System That Never Fails by William Clement Stone, and The Greatest Salesman by Og Mandino. All three books inspired me, and gave me a new perspective about success. I also bought the book, Cosmic Consciousness, which deals with the study of the Universe, and I read about the human aura, which Dr. Kirlian, a Russian scientist, was able to photograph. Likewise, I learned that each organ in our body has a specific energy which is the basis for magnetic resonance imaging. I spent the whole night reading these books and didn't feel tired from the lack of sleep.

Several years later, I had a patient with abdominal cancer. I told the patient that there was nothing else I could do to help him. He called me several times to beg me to operate on him. His eating habits were good. He didn't seem to have lost any weight. Eventually, I scheduled him and while I was scrubbing my hands, I prayed that the good Lord would do the surgery and that He would just use my hands. After I made the incision, I explored the entire abdomen, which was full of cancer. Suddenly, I felt that my right hand was held steadily and all of the cancer cells were falling like pebbles into my hand. Masterfully, the specimen container was filled with cancer cells and the abdomen was noted to be clear of tumors. The patient lived for ten more years. These experiences absolutely proved to me the existence of a powerful and loving God. It was the most rewarding and unforgettable event in which I witnessed that God's healing power still exists today.

A book I recently read, The Ministry of Healing, affirmed that health providers, especially doctors and nurses, should and must take the good Lord as their partner in treating or healing their patients. After all, Jesus Christ is the same yesterday, today and forever. (Hebrew 13:8.) He is the source of life, wisdom, and the greatest physician.

As a poor, teenage boy in my hometown in the Philippines, to go to college seemed an impossible dream. Medical school was even more impossible due to the long years and expensive tuition. Unlike the United States where there are several grants and student loans available, my homeland offered no loans. My determination to overcome all adversities and to surmount all difficult barriers eventually enabled me to graduate from Manila Central University on April 15, 1958. After graduating from college, I spent three years doing charity work in Bambang, Nueva Vizcaya, Philippines. I saw many patients every day: These were the patients who could not afford to see a doctor or buy their own medicine. There was a rural health physician, but he was too busy: He sold his medicine to his patients rather than giving it to them free. There were no Medicaid or Welfare programs in our country. The feeling I got from being able to help them gave me enormous joy. My patients became my best friends.

During those three years of general medical practice, I came into contact with patients who needed surgery beyond my expertise. I knew then that I needed additional medical training, so I moved to the United States to pursue training in general surgery including thoracic and cardiovascular surgery at the Long Island Jewish Hospital in New Hyde Park, New York, and Queens Hospital Center in Jamaica, New York.

After my training was complete, I moved to West Virginia and worked at Roane General Hospital in Spencer. At that time, it was a newly built medical center. My services were very much needed in 1969. I worked there until my retirement from private practice on April 4, 1994 due to illness. After two years, I recovered and I went back to work at an outpatient clinic and later as a medical director and staff physician in nursing homes for four years before retiring again. During my years of medical and surgical practice, the Lord used my hands in many difficult surgeries for which I am eternally grateful.

The Lord has been very good to me. In my search to do something that would please Him, I decided to review the Ten Commandments. In this book, I have made several quotations about the blessings of the righteous, the rewards of the faithful, and the punishment of the violators of His laws. The rest of this book highlights my experiences as a doctor, as a man of faith, and as an author. As a doctor, I have observed that physical health is invariably connected to the mental, emotional, and spiritual health. It is these principles that have inspired me to write, with the hope that my readers will be inspired and empowered to change their lives for the better.

The articles in this book are not a novel or targeted to one particular group of readers. My orientation as a physician is mainly writing prescriptions. Hence, my articles are short, yet simple, clear instructions to kindle a change in the behavior of my readers for good.

Chapter 1
God's Greatest Prescription for the Human Race
An introduction about the Ten Commandments

The Ten Commandments are a great prescription designed for the benefit and welfare of mankind. This prescription is the greatest prescription of all because it is unchangeable, eternal, and powerful. The Ten Commandments are the vital ingredients of the Bible. They are like the Constitution of the United States of America, as the guiding principles to govern this wonderful country and her people righteously in order that peace and order may be established. If followed faithfully, solemnly and with prayer, they will bring joy; happiness, good health, long life, and even wealth. If people only understood this truth, they would exhaust all methods to obtain and follow this prescription.

This prescription has always been available. All the treasures of life and the guiding principles of life are clearly written in the Bible. The reason this prescription is so unique and powerful is because it is inspired by God, the Creator of the Universe. It was handed down to everyone. Jesus Christ advised us to follow faithfully and without any precondition or reservation. When God created the human race, He intended for man to live peacefully, to love God with all our strength, heart, and mind, and to love one another. God made this clear to us through His words. The Ten Commandments are simple and easy to understand. They enable us to identify God's will.

Wouldn't it be nice if there were no murderers, thieves, or liars? Unfortunately, these do exist. People who exhibit these behaviors disobey God and violate His commandments. The consequences result in the world in which we live today.

Even though there are some people who do not know God, most people do believe in Him. Some either don't know His commandments or they choose not to obey them. The Bible says that the violation of one commandment is a violation of them all. The commandments connect our relationship to God with our relationship to each other. When one commandment is broken, it is disobedience to the will of God as shown in James 2:10 *"For whoever shall keep the whole law, and yet offend in one point, he is guilty of all."* Leviticus 20:22 *"You shall therefore keep all my statutes, and all my judgments, and do them that the land whither I bring you to dwell therein, spue you not out."*

It is my belief that most people want to be good and they want to be members of the true family of God. To achieve this, they need motivation, strong faith, and a constant reminder that following the Ten Commandments is the way to live in order to achieve success, live a long life, and attain happiness.

The Lord mentioned in the book of Deuteronomy 11:18-20 *"Therefore shall he lay up these my words in your heart and in your Soul, and bind them for a sign upon your hand, that they may be as frontlets between your eyes. And you shall teach them your children, speaking of them when thou sittest in thine house, and when thou walkest by the way, when thou liest down, and thou risest up. And thou shalt write them upon the doorpost of thine house and upon thy gates."*

Sometime ago, I asked the Lord what I could do for Him. In a mysterious way, I felt called to have this poster made with the aid of an artist, Mr. Rodney Miller. This came after I had reviewed the Ten Commandments. This Ten Commandment poster placed in your home will act as an angel reminding you how important it is to obey God's laws so that we may be rewarded with many blessings and prove that we truly love Him.

John 14:21 says: *"He that hath my commandments, and keepeth them, he it is that loveth me: and he that loveth me shall be loved of my Father; and I will love him, and will manifest myself to him."* Complete obedience and fulfillment of the will and commandments of God are proofs that we love Jesus Christ.

Matthew 16:26 states: *"For what is a man profited, if he shall gain the whole world, and lose his own soul? Or what shall a man give in exchange for his soul?"*

Other Scriptures on the importance of the Ten Commandments include:

John 14:15 *"If ye love me, keep my commandments."*

John 15:7 *"If ye abide in me, and my words abide in you, ye shall ask what ye will, and it shall be done unto you."*

Deuteronomy 8:11 *"Beware that thou forget not the Lord thy God, in not keeping his commandments, and his Judgments, and his statutes, which I command thee this day."*

Deuteronomy 8:6 *"Therefore thou shall keep the commandments of the Lord thy God, to walk in His ways and to fear Him."*

I am aware that most of the rituals described in the Old Testament may have been abolished. There is one thing that I am confused about and that is the verse found in St. Matthews 5:17-18 *"Think not that I am come to destroy the law or the prophets; I am not come to destroy, but to fulfill. For verily I say unto you, till heaven and earth pass, one jot or one title shall in no wise pass from the law till all be fulfilled."* It states further in Verse 19: *"Whosoever therefore shall break one of these least commandments, and shall teach men so, he shall be called the least in the kingdom of heaven; but whosoever shall do and teach them, the same shall be called great in the kingdom of heaven."* St. Matthews 24:34-35 states: *"Verily I say unto you, this generation shall not pass till all these things be fulfilled. Heaven and earth shall pass away, but my words shall not pass away."* Jesus Christ fulfilled the law, but it is my belief that we human beings must also fulfill the law.

All of the verses quoted above strengthen my beliefs that God's commandments, precepts, teachings, and rules are unchangeable, indestructible, and eternal.

The Greatest Prescription

Chapter 2
The Ten Commandments

Exodus 20:1-17 (KJV)

I. *Thou shalt have no other gods before me.*

II. *Thou shalt not make unto thee any graven image, or any likeness of anything that is in heaven above, or that is in the earth beneath, or that is in the water under the earth. You shall not bow down to them, for I the Lord your God, am a jealous God, punishing children for the iniquity of parents, to the third generations of those who rejected me, but showing steadfast love to thousand generations of those who love me and keep my commandments.*

III. *Thou shalt not take the name of the Lord thy God in vain; for the Lord will not hold him guiltless that taketh his name in vain.*

IV. *Remember the Sabbath Day, to keep it holy. Six days shall thou labour and do all thy work, but the seventh day is the Sabbath of the Lord thy God, in it thou shall not do any work, nor thy son, nor thy daughter, nor thy manservant, nor thy maidservant, nor thy cattle, nor thy stranger within thy gates.*

V. *Honour thy father and thy mother; that thy days may be long upon the land which the Lord thy God giveth thee.*

VI. *Thou shalt not kill.*

VII. *Thou shalt not commit adultery*

VIII. *Thou shalt not steal.*

IX.   Thou shalt not bear false witness against thy neighbour.
X.   Thou shalt not covet thy neighbor's house, thou shalt not covet they neighbour's wife, nor his manservant, nor his maidservant, nor his ox, nor his ass, nor anything that is thy neighbour's.

Other verses to remember include:

Ecclesiastes 12: 13 *"Let us hear the conclusion of the whole matter: Fear God and keep his commandments, for this is the whole duty of man."*

Matthew 22:37-40 *"Jesus said unto him, 'Thou shalt love the Lord thy God with all thy heart, and with all thy soul, and with all thy mind. This is the first and great commandment. And the second is like unto it, Thou shalt love thy neighbor as thyself. On these two commandments hang all the law and the prophets."*

Deuteronomy 6: 17 *"Ye shall diligently keep the commandments of the Lord your God and his testimonies, and his statutes, which he hath commanded thee."*

Deuteronomy 8: 3 *"And he humbled thee, and suffered thee to hunger; and fed thee with manna, which thou knewest not, neither did thy fathers know; that he might make thee know that man doth not live by bread only, but by every word that proceedeth out of the mouth of the Lord doth man live."*

Deuteronomy 10: 12-13 *"And now Israel, what doth the Lord thy God require of thee, but to fear the Lord thy God, to walk in his ways, and to love him, and to serve the Lord thy God with all thy heart and with all thy soul, to keep the commandments of the Lord, and his statutes, which I command thee this day for thy good?"*

Deuteronomy 8: 11 *"Beware that thou forget not the Lord thy God, in not keeping his commandments, and his judgments, and his statutes, which I command thee this day."*

Romans 13: 8-9 *"Owe no man anything, but to love one another; for he that loveth another hath fulfilled the law. For this, Thou shalt not commit adultery, Thou shalt not kill, Thou shalt not steal, Thou shalt not bear false witness, Thou shalt not covet, and if there be any other commandment, it is briefly comprehended in this saying, namely, Thou shalt love thy neighbor as thyself."*

Psalm 19:7-10 *"The law of the Lord is perfect, converting the soul, the testimony of the Lord is sure, making wise the simple. The statutes of the Lord are right, rejoicing the heart; the commandment of the Lord is pure, enlightening the eyes. The fear of the Lord is clean, enduring forever; the judgments of the Lord are true and righteous altogether. More to be desired are they than gold, yea, than much fine gold, sweeter also than honey and the honeycomb."*

Psalm 119: This entire chapter tells more about the laws and precepts of God and commandments of God.

1 Kings 2:2-3 *"I go the way of all the earth; be thou strong therefore, and shew thyself a man. And keep the charge of the Lord thy God, to walk in his ways, to keep his statutes, and his commandments, and his judgments, and his testimonies, as it is written in the law of Moses, that thou mayest prosper in all that thou doest, and whithersoever thou turnest thyself."*

Proverbs 3: 1-4 *"My son, forget not my law but let thine heart keep my commandments; for length of days, and long life, and peace, shall they add to thee. Let not mercy and truth forsake thee; bind them about thy neck; write them upon the table of thine heart. So shalt thou find favour and good understanding in the sight of God and man."*

Proverbs 7:1-3 *"My son, keep my words, and lay up my commandments with thee. Keep my commandments, and live; and my law as the apple of thine eye. Bind them upon thy fingers, write them upon the table of thine heart."*

Proverbs 13:13 *"Whoso despiseth the word shall be destroyed, but he that feareth the commandment shall be rewarded."*

Matthew 5: 17-20 *"Think not that I am come to destroy the law or the prophets. I am not come to destroy, but to fulfill. For verily I say unto you, till heaven and earth pass, one jot or one title shall in no wise pass from the law till all be fulfilled. Whosoever therefore shall break one of these least commandments, and shall teach men so, he shall be called the least in the kingdom of heaven; but whosoever shall do and teach them, the same shall be called great in the kingdom of heaven. For I say unto you, that except your righteousness shall exceed the righteousness of the scribes and Pharisees, ye shall in no case enter into the kingdom of heaven."*

Matthew 12:29-31 *"Or else, how can one enter into a strong man's house, and spoil his goods, except he first bind the strong man? And then he will spoil his house. He that is not with me is against me; and he that gathereth not with me scattereth abroad. Wherefore I say unto you, all manner of sin and blasphemy shall be forgiven unto men, but the blasphemy against the Holy Ghost shall not be forgiven unto men."*

John 14:15-16 *"If ye love me, keep my commandments. And I will pray the Father; and he shall give you another Comforter; that he may abide with you forever."*

John 14: 21, 23 *"He that hath my commandments, and keepeth them, he it is that loveth me; and he that loveth me shall be loved of my Father; and I will love him, and will manifest myself to him. Jesus answered and said unto him, if a man love me, he will keep my words; and my Father will love him, and we will come unto him, and make our abode with him."*

John 15:10-11 *"If ye keep my commandments, ye shall abide in my love; even as I have kept my Father's commandments, and abide in his love. These things have I spoken unto you, that my joy might remain in you, and that your joy might be full."*

Punishments of the Violators

Deuteronomy 28:15-31 *"But it shall come to pass, if thou wilt not hearken unto the voice of Lord thy God, to observe to do all his commandments and his statutes which I command thee this day; that all these curses shall come upon thee, and overtake thee; Cursed shalt thou be in the city, and cursed shalt thou be in the field. Cursed shall be thy basket and thy store. Cursed shall be the fruit of thy body, and the fruit of thy land, the increase of thy kine, and the flocks of thy sheep. Cursed shalt thou be when thou comest in, and cursed shalt thou be when thou goest out. The Lord shall send upon thee cursing, vexation, and rebuke, in all that thou settest thine hand unto for to do, until thou perish quickly; because of wickedness of thy doings, whereby thou hast forsaken me. The Lord shall make the pestilence cleave unto thee, until he have consumed thee from off the land, whither thou goest to possess it. The Lord shall smite thee with a consumption, and with a fever; and with an inflammation, and with an extreme burning, and with the sword, and with blasting, and with mildew; and they shall pursue thee until thou perish. And thy heaven that is over thy head shall be brass, and the earth that is under thee shall be iron. The Lord shall make the rain of thy land powder and dust; from heaven shall it come down upon thee, until thou be destroyed. The Lord shall cause thee to be smitten before thine enemies; thou shalt go out one way against them, and flee seven ways before them; and shalt be removed into all the kingdoms of the earth. And thy carcass shall be meat unto all fowls of the air and unto the beasts of the earth, and no man shall fray them away. The Lord will smite thee with the botch of Egypt, and with the emerods, and with the scab, and with the itch, whereof thou canst not be healed. The Lord shall smite thee with madness, and blindness, and astonishment of heart. And thou shalt grope at noonday, as the blind gropeth in darkness, and thou shalt not prosper in thy ways, and thou shalt be only oppressed and spoiled evermore, and no man shall save thee. Thou shalt betroth a wife, and another man shall lie with her; thou shalt build a house, and thou shalt not dwell therein; thou shalt plant a vineyard, and shalt not gather the grapes thereof. Thine ox shall be slain before thine eyes, and thou shalt not eat thereof; thine ass shall be violently taken away from before thy face, and shall not be restored to thee; thy sheep shall be given unto thine enemies, and thou shalt have none to rescue them."*

Leviticus 26:14-33 *"But if ye will not hearken unto me, and will not do all these commandments, and if ye shall despise my statutes, or if your soul abhor my judgments, so that ye will not do all my commandments, but that ye break my covenant, I also will do this unto you; I will even appoint over you terror, consumption, and the burning ague, that shall consume the eyes, and cause sorrow of heart. And ye shall sow your seed in vain, for your enemies shall eat it. And I will set my face against you, and ye shall be slain before your enemies. They that hate you shall reign over you, and ye shall flee when none pursueth you. And if ye will not yet for all this hearken unto me, then I will punish you seven times more for your sins. And I will break the pride of your power, and I will make your heaven as iron, and your earth as brass, and your strength shall be spent in vain; for your land shall not yield her increase, neither shall the trees of the land yield their fruits. And if ye walk contrary unto me, and will not hearken unto me, I will bring seven times more plagues upon you, according to your sins. I will also send wild beasts among you, which shall rob you of your children, and destroy your cattle, and make you few in number; and your highways shall be desolate. And if ye will not be reformed by me by these things, but will walk contrary unto me, then will I also walk contrary unto you, and will punish you yet seven times for your sins. And I will bring a sword upon you that shall avenge the quarrel of my covenant; and when ye are gathered together within your cities, I will send the pestilence among you; and ye shall be delivered into the hand of the enemy. And when I have broken the staff of your bread, ten women shall bake your bread in one oven, and they shall deliver you your bread again by weight, and ye shall eat and not be satisfied. And if ye will not for this hearken unto me, but walk contrary unto me, then I will walk contrary unto you also in fury; and even I, will chastise you seven times for your sins. And ye shall eat the flesh of your sons, and the flesh of your daughters shall ye eat. And I will destroy your high places, and cut down your images, and cast your carcass upon the carcass of your idols, and my soul shall abhor you. And I will make your cities waste, and bring your sanctuaries unto desolation, and I will not smell the savour of your sweet odours. And I will bring the land into desolation, and your enemies which dwell therein shall be astonished at it. And I will scatter you among the heathen, and will draw out a sword after you; and your land shall be desolate, and your cities waste."*

Rewards of the Righteous

Deuteronomy 7:12-15 *"Wherefore it shall come to pass, if ye hearken to these judgments, and keep and do them, that the Lord thy God shall keep unto thee the covenant and the mercy which he sware unto thy fathers. And he will love thee, and bless thee, and multiply thee; he will also bless the fruit of thy womb, and the fruit of thy land, thy corn, and thy wine, and thine oil, the increase of thy kine, and the flocks of thy sheep, in the land which he sware unto thy fathers to give thee. Thou shalt be blessed above all people; there shall not be male or female barren among you, or among your cattle. And the Lord will take away from thee all sickness, and will put none of the evil diseases of Egypt, which thou knowest, upon thee, but will lay them upon all them that hate thee."*

Deuteronomy 11:8-9 *"Therefore shall ye keep all the commandments which I command you this day, that ye may be strong, and go in and possess the land, whither ye go to possess it; And that ye may prolong your days in the land, which the Lord sware unto your fathers to give unto them and to their seed, a land that floweth with milk and honey."*

Deuteronomy 11:13-15 *"And it shall come to pass, if ye shall hearken diligently unto my commandments which I command you this day, to love the Lord your God, and to serve him with all your heart and with all your soul, That I will give you the rain of your land in due season, the first rain and the latter rain, that thou mayest gather in thy corn, and thy wine, and thine oil. And I will send grass in thy fields for thy cattle, that thou mayest eat and be full."*

Deuteronomy 11:18-19 *"Therefore shall ye lay up these my words in your heart and in your soul, and bind them for a sign upon your hand, that they may be as frontlets between your eyes. And ye shall teach them your children, speaking of them when thou sittest in thine house, and when thou walkest by the way, when thou liest down, and when thou risest up."*

Deuteronomy 11:20-25 *"And thou shalt write them upon the doorposts of thine house, and upon thy gates, that your days may be multiplied, and the days of your children, in the land which the Lord swore unto your fathers to give them, as the days of heaven upon the earth. For if ye shall diligently keep all these commandments which I command you, to do them, to love the Lord your God, to walk in all his ways, and to cleave unto him; then will the Lord drive out all these nations from before you, and ye shall possess greater nations and mightier than yourselves. Every place whereon the soles of your feet shall tread shall be yours; from the wilderness and Lebanon, from the river; the river Euphrates, even unto the uttermost sea shall your coast be. There shall no man be able to stand before you; for the Lord your God shall lay the fear of you and the dread of you upon all the land that ye shall tread upon, as he hath said unto you."*

Leviticus 26:3-5 *"If ye walk in my statutes, and keep my commandments, and do them; then I will give you rain in due season, and the land shall yield her increase, and the trees of the field shall yield their fruit. And your threshing shall reach unto the vintage, and the vintage shall reach them unto the sowing time; and ye shall eat your bread to the full, and dwell in your land safely."*

Leviticus 26:9 *"For I will have respect unto you, and make you fruitful, and multiply you, and establish my covenant with you."*

Leviticus 26:11-12 *"And I will set my tabernacle among you; and my soul shall not abhor you. And I will walk among you, and will be your God, and ye shall be my people."*

Proverbs 19: 16 *"He that keepeth the commandment keepeth his own soul; but he that despiseth his ways shall die."*

Psalm 112:1-10 *"Praise ye the Lord. Blessed is the man that feareth the Lord that delighteth greatly in his commandments. His seed shall be mighty upon the earth; the generation of the upright shall be blessed, wealth and riches shall be in his house, and his righteousness endureth forever: Unto the upright there ariseth light in the darkness; he is gracious, and full of compassion, and righteous. A good man showeth favor; and lendeth; he will guide his affairs with discretion. Surely he shall not be moved forever; the righteous shall be in everlasting remembrance. He shall not be afraid of evil tidings; his heart is fixed, trusting in the Lord. His heart is established, he shall not be afraid, until he see his desire upon his enemies. He hath dispersed, he hath given to the poor; his righteousness endureth forever; his horn shall be exalted with honor. The wicked shall see it, and be grieved; he shall gnash his teeth, and melt away; the desire of the wicked shall perish."*

John 3: 16, 36 *"For God so loved the world, that he gave his only begotten Son, that whosoever believeth in him should not perish, but have everlasting life. He that believeth in the Son hath everlasting life; and he that believeth not the Son shall not see life; but the wrath of God abideth on him."*

John 11:25-26 *"Jesus said unto her: 'I am the resurrection, and the life; he that believeth in me, though he were dead, yet shall he live. And whosoever liveth and believeth in me shall never die. Believest thou this?"*

The verses in this book are quoted from the New International Version, Copyright 1990 by Zondervan Corporation with permission and from the King James Version published by The World Publishing Company; New York.

Chapter 3
My Best Prescription

Shortly after I settled in Spencer, West Virginia, I took time to read my Bible and attended church regularly, including Bible class every Sunday. I wrote a sermon entitled, "My Best and Greatest Prescription." I wish now that I had recorded my entire sermon then. I made an outline and explained every paragraph. The outline is as follows:

New life is begun by accepting Jesus Christ as your Creator and Savior. Ask for the forgiveness of your sins and love God with all your heart, mind, and soul. Pray that others will do the same. Include your enemies in your prayers.

Learn the commandments of God and His teachings. Apply them every moment of your life as the guiding principles in the conduct of your affairs with your fellow humans. God states in the Book of St. John 14: 15 *"If you love me, you will keep my commandments."*

I know that your thoughts and ideas are who you are 99 percent of the time while your acts, whether noble or otherwise, make up the remaining one percent. This is so because every decision made starts first as an idea or thought followed by an action. Perhaps the greatest challenge every day is having right thoughts. If we do not control those that are not pleasant or righteous, we suffer consequences. If we do the right thing, we will be rewarded with many good things. I believe it is important not to dwell on thoughts that are not consistent with the Divine principles or in harmony with our governmental laws or we may execute those unrighteous acts. Unfortunately, no matter how close we are to God, we experience more difficulties. I also believe that the hardships that we suffer are a test of our patience and faith to God.

Remember what the Bible says in the Book of Proverbs: *"As a man thinketh in his heart so is he."* Matthew 5:27-28 states that anyone who looks at a woman with lust has already committed adultery.

Don't take your body for granted; special care for your physical body ensures that your earthly temple-where your thoughts and soul are stored is healthy. Visit your physician regularly, follow healthy habits, and maintain healthy nutrition and exercise habits so that you may live healthier and longer.

Wake up every morning with a fresh outlook on life, a grateful heart, and a noble mind filled with beautiful thoughts and ideas. Plan your activities for the day. Anticipate what you are going to do. Imagine good results. Be prepared to accept challenges, opportunities, and blessings. Resolve to do all the good works you can do today. While tomorrow may never come, look forward to a brighter, more challenging and rewarding day. Affirm that you are the most blessed person alive because you were born a champion. Don't doubt yourself. Believe that you were born to succeed and to receive good things because the Lord is with you and if you are with Him, all things are possible. Remember what St. Luke 18:27 says: *"The things which are impossible with men are possible with God."* KJV. *"I can do all things through Christ which strengthens me."* (Philippians 4: 13)

Try to forget the worries, problems, loneliness, fears, and negative thoughts in the valley of oblivion. Erase them from your mind and substitute them with love, understanding, faith, and confidence. Work on patience and enthusiasm, which are the great dynamic virtues because they enrich our lives. Thank God for the ordeals and miseries you have encountered. They are the springboards of humility. They are the bridges and magnetic forces that bring you closer to God. Realize that problems and worries are blessings rather than burdens; they should serve as inspirations rather than failures.

Remember that genuine happiness is something that one cannot buy borrow, or transfer. It is created within and it is the expression of a dynamic faith. It acts as a generator to move one's life with vigor and vivacity: Joy makes the heart and mind sing in perfect harmony: It is the expression of one's attunement with God. It is the expression of satisfaction, peace, and good health in both the material and spiritual world. Read also on my topic "Prescription for Happiness" elsewhere in this book.

Remember that true wealth is kept in one's grateful heart, filled with infinite love. Real riches are one's thoughtful mind, beautiful thoughts, and wisdom. This is expressed through cheerful smiles, tender words, and noble deeds.

Search for divine and human wisdom that help to unravel the mysteries of life so you can better understand and better serve God, others, and yourself.

Chapter 4
Timeless Principles in Achieving True "SUCCESS"

SUCCESS: It's what everyone wants to be or have. But, what is the real meaning of success? To an athlete, success is winning a gold medal at the Olympics; to a doctor, success is reviving a patient from cardiac arrest; to a businessman, success is building a prosperous enterprise; and to a lawyer, it is defending a client in a difficult case.

I often read of rich people that are miserable despite their fortune. They don't understand the importance of how to handle their fortune. For example, King Solomon, who had all the wealth on earth, ruled a very large kingdom, built temples layered with gold, and received valuable gifts from different kings and queens. He was eventually punished by God because he acquired seven hundred wives, three hundred concubines, and was persuaded to worship false gods. His kingdom was divided into smaller kingdoms and given to other kings. See 1 Kings, Chapter 3-11.

While wealth can bring many good things such as building schools and churches, providing scholarships to deserving students, and donating money to different charities, it may also cause a lot of problems. Example: There was a person who won several million dollars in a lottery. He was "scammed" many times, his granddaughter was lulled, and even his wife divorced him. He built pizza parlors, but became bankrupt. He ended up losing all the money that he had won.

A similar experience happened to King Nebuchadnezzar who ruled the world. He was thrown from his kingdom and went to live in the forest of Babylon with beasts. This occurred because he forced his people to kneel and worship the tall, golden tower that he built. Read the Book of Daniel.

There have been many recent happenings that echo the events described in the Old Testament. In 1999, the U.S. economy saw tremendous growth. There were many companies, including dotcoms, where their businesses grew. This allowed many people to make millions-even billions-only to become bankrupt at the end of 2000 and 2001. An example of this is the Enron Company which claimed to have $80 billion in assets only to declare bankruptcy a year later. As a result, employees lost their savings and pension plans. The investors of the company suffered financial difficulties.

Since 2001, the economy has decreased. What was once thought to have been a surplus of several billion dollars only a few years ago, has now been converted into a deficit. Likewise, the value of the dollar has come down.

I have seen mansions destroyed by floods, hurricanes, and fire. I have known people who have died young because of their bad habits. Some people believe that Hurricanes Andrew and Katrina could be the result of the government not allowing the Ten Commandments to be displayed or allowing legalized abortions.

I have friends who became rich but are sick and unhappy because their children are drug addicts and have abandoned the family. Some went to school but did not finish because of poor discipline. These things were not and are not indicators of true success.

My personal definition of success or wealth means making life better for yourself and for your family. Good health or wealth does not only mean the physical well being, but also one's financial, mental, emotional, and spiritual wellness. It is a life that is well balanced and that fulfills all of one's priorities and responsibilities, including faith in God, the Source of life, and numerous blessings.

God is the Creator of the Universe and the fullness thereof. He is the Creator of our lives and provides us with all of the things that we need and other numerous blessings that we can never count or realize.

1 Kings 2:2-3 *"I go the way of all the earth; be thou strong therefore, and show thyself a man; and keep the charge of the Lord thy God, to walk in*

his ways, to keep his statutes, and his commandments, and his judgments, and his testimonies, as it is written in the law of Moses, that thou mayest prosper in all that thou doest, and whithersoever thou turnest thyself

Deuteronomy 8: 11 *"But remember the Lord your God, for it is He who gives you power to get wealth so that He may confirm His covenant (promise) that He swore to your ancestor that he is doing today."*

I believe that success is an ongoing process that consistently defines your life in harmony with God's will.

So, then, how can we achieve success? Select a career. This is important because you will theoretically or in reality be doing this for the rest of your life. The career that you choose should serve your greatest interests, and reflect your talents. My passion was to be able to help the poor and sick people with the help of God. Financial obstacles can be overcome when the goal is in harmony with God's will or plan. As soon as you have chosen a profession, the next step is to determine how to achieve the goal.

Working toward a goal is like a journey; one must have a starting point and continue on through obstacles until reaching the destination. It is also like the work of an architect who must draw vividly and descriptively the plans and follow through in the process of building a home. Architects must also arrange the proper workers and tools to complete a task; likewise, a successful career requires these seven tools:

S **Setting the Right Goal**. The right goal is that which is achievable based on an individual's greatest interest and his/her natural abilities. You cannot possibly become an engineer if you hate math, nor can you become a doctor if the sight of blood makes you woozy. Your career goal should be written very specifically with a projected date of completion. The latter is very important because, if you do not have a timeframe, you are bound to procrastinate and you will never succeed.

U **Understanding**. You must completely understand all stages and details of your plan. You must make it clear in your written plan, and to yourself, that one step of the plan must be completed before moving on to the next step. Learn about the different obstacles that may possibly hinder you so that you may be prepared. Also, make sure that you are aware that you may need the help of others to complete your career journey.

The Bible tells us to ask for wisdom; James 1:5 advises us on seeking God's help: "*If any of you lack wisdom, let him ask of God that giveth to all men liberally, and upbraideth not; and it shall be given him.*" Also, see Proverbs 16:3, which says: "*Commit thy work unto the Lord, and thy plans shall be established.*" Psalm 32:8 has insight on this subject, too: "*I will instruct thee and teach thee in the way which thou shalt go. I will guide thee with mine eye.*" Despite the above verse, if you fail, do not give up. Continue to look for solution.

C   **Concentrate**. Focus your thoughts on the various stages and visualize the best solutions. Focus on the plans that allow you to follow through. You may also think of more ideas to speed the process along. While this is important, do not forget to perform your priorities and responsibilities to God, your family, your church, and your community.

C   **Conscientious**. Be aware that dedication, hard work, and perseverance will enable you to succeed no matter how difficult your situation. Remember that for every problem encountered there is an equivalent opportunity; and know that all problems are only temporary. Eventually, they are resolved and better options may become available. In other words, strengthen your faith. Don't ever give up. Matthew 17:20 states: "*And Jesus said unto them, "Because of your unbelief; for verily I say unto you, ye have faith as a grain of mustard seed, ye shall say unto this mountain," Remove hence to yonder place, and it shall removed and nothing shall be impossible to you.*"

E   **Enthusiasm and Relentless Patience**. Always maintain your enthusiasm and your optimism. Mental engineering or visualization has various benefits that can help you overcome stress and anxieties. Positive thoughts will help you generate ideas that will help you hasten the realization of your goal. "*But they that wait upon the Lord shall renew their strength, they shall mount up with wings as eagles, they shall run and not be weary, they shall walk and not faint.*" (Isaiah 40:31) Therefore, be patient.

S   **Strengthen**. Strengthen your pleasant attitudes, your knowledge, and many other areas, including your health. Remember that education is a lifetime journey Learning is very important because it allows you to adapt yourself to improving technology; which, in turn, will improve your career or business. Take good care of your body by eating the right foods, such as fruits, vegetables, grains, and lean meats. Get adequate rest as well as exercise. Visit your physician periodically for thorough check-ups. Ask your doctor about the things you should do in order to maintain excellent health! We are prone to develop illnesses as we grow old, but if we take care of our body; we may live longer and more comfortably.

S   **Service**. Dedicate yourself to excellent service. Always be courteous, friendly, generous, and helpful. These attitudes will propel you to prosperity. Don't allow yourself to be arrogant or boastful, for these negative characteristics will only bring you down. Proverbs 16:5: "*Every one that is proud in heart is an abomination to the Lord.*" Always remember God. Donate your time or money to your church or other charitable organizations. Gratitude is shown to God when you help the needy God gives you the power to achieve your wealth and success.

Review Deuteronomy 8: 11 Always be faithful to Him. Learn and apply all His teachings and commandments.

Proverbs 3: 1-2 states: "*My son, forget not my law; but let thine heart keep my commandments; for length of days, and long lift, and peace, shall they add to thee.*"

Matthew 16:26 "*For what is a man profited, if he shall gain the whole world and lose his own soul? Or what shall a man give in exchange for his soul?*" Mark 11:24: "*So, I tell you whatever you ask for in prayer; believed that you have received and it will be yours.*"

1 John 5: 14 "*If we ask anything according to His will, He hears us.*"

Matthew 6: 7-8 "*Ask and it shall be given you, seek and you shall find.*"

Matthew 6:32-33 "*Seek ye first the kingdom of God and His righteousness and all these things shall be added unto you.*"

Philippians 4:13 "*I can do all things through Christ who strengthens me.*"

Chapter 5
Other Thoughts on Success

Over the years, I learned that success could be defined in many ways (please see the previous chapter for my definitions of success). In my own personal thinki.ng, success may be summarized in two words: good relationships. I believe that good relationships are the basis for a successful life. What good is it if you don't have a pleasant relationship with yourself, your family; your neighbors, your community, or God? Good relationships are all about love, unity, cooperation, participation, good times, pleasures, commitments, loyalty, and trust. These virtues are the unbreakable ties that make good relationships in both good and critical circumstances. No matter how intelligent or brilliant you are, no matter how many degrees you have earned, if you don't nurture good relationships, your knowledge is of no value and you are a failure.

How can one be in a good relationship with one's self? What are the attributes of an individual? I believe that each person is made up of three parts: a body which is the physical part; a mind that governs the physical part; and a spirit, which is responsible for our being alive.

There are many books about the connections among the mind, body, and spirit. It is the powerful spirit, which is responsible for our state of being alive, which God breathed into our nostrils. Without the spirit, the physical body is dead, regardless of the cause, whether it is due to severe trauma or sickness. Some mistake it as the soul.

When God created mankind, He formed the body', breathed into his nostrils, and he became a living soul (Genesis 2:7). The soul constitutes the mind, body, and spirit. Although we are one person, why do I say that an individual can be more than one? In other words, perhaps it is simpler to say that each individual has two major personalities: One represents the carnal body made of flesh, which we call the ego, and the other part represents the spiritual or divine part.

The ego desires pleasure whether right or wrong, while the spiritual aspect desires what is righteous, noble, and harmless. The problem with mankind is that the ego overpowers the spiritual and, if this happens, the individual may become harmful to himself and others. The ego has the characteristics of greed, selfishness, covetousness, and arrogance, which are all against divine principles. If allowed to go unbalanced or to become dominant in our life, the ego may lead us to have a miserable failure. One may suffer depression, anxiety (with or without a panic disorder), confusion, or psychosis. Sometimes, the individual is subject to a variety of stresses, which may lead to a depressed immunity leading to a variety of diseases such as cancer, infections leading to septicemia, shock, and death.

On the contrary, spiritual life exists on divine principles. If one's spirit is aligned with God, then good things are one's birthright. All God's attributes are noble, commendable, lawful, pleasant, and beneficial. To be in harmony or in good relationship to one's self, the ego has to surrender itself to the spiritual aspect. This is done by changing one's thoughts and, subsequently, all actions. One should take an inventory of all bad things, bad thoughts, and bad habits. Bad thoughts must be eliminated from one's mind. Thoughts can be controlled. Therefore, when we change our thoughts, we can change our actions, habits, and character. Good thoughts, habits, and attributes, like compassion, generosity, cooperation, faithfulness, enthusiasm, positive thinking, and obedience to governmental and divine laws must be reinforced. These attributes can be strengthened by practicing them consistently.

Next, you must constantly evaluate your relationship with your parents, siblings, spouse, and children. When we were children, we knew that good relationships meant obeying our parents, being cooperative, helpful, sharing, and loving. When we became adults, our responsibilities increased. When we have children, then we must provide not only the basics like food, shelter, and safety, but also leadership, support emotional, mental, spiritual, and financially and education. Helping your spouse care for your children is essential. Children need positive influences from both parents. Take your children to church. Teach them about God. Teach them to know the difference between right and wrong. Play games with them. Encourage them to join groups that nurture their interests such as Boy Scouts, Girl Scouts, the 4H Club, or other community groups.

It is likewise important that you help your spouse with everything that needs to be done. Share responsibilities such as washing the dishes, cleaning the house, doing the laundry and even preparing a healthy breakfast. Sometimes it takes a lot of sacrifices to maintain excellent relationships within the family and with others. You may take your family to a concert or movie. Take them to their favorite restaurants for their birthdays. Give your children incentives with a few dollars or other gifts that you know they will enjoy Give your wife beautiful roses every now and then.

Relationships with your friends and neighbors are fostered simply by the practice of the Golden Rule. Relationships make it easier to ask for help. It is through good will, honesty, and trust that good relationships are established. Neighbors don't know each other as well as they did in the past. Isolation from neighbors brings no good. Get together with them to know more about each other. Schedule a small party like a watermelon party, or invite them for a pizza, or bake them a batch of your specialty cookies. Some neighbors are too ashamed to discuss things with other neighbors. Maybe one could ask what they could do to help them or if they know of someone that needs help.

Good relationships extend to your place of employment or business. These relationships require patience, understanding, compassion, and unselfish devotion. I know employees who perform beyond their job duties. They clean the floors, throwaway the garbage, and even stay to work late. They are very responsible and caring.

Good relationships within your community, church, and other organizations also require some of these same attributes along with volunteerism, cooperation, and support for worthy goals and activities. You will learn about community problems and projects by participating in the Chamber of Commerce, Rotary Club, or Lion's Club.

Good relationships with your co-creatures, such as birds, wild animals, etc., are fostered by a love and appreciation for the environment. You can set out birdseed in the winter and protect stray animals. While visiting our daughter in Chang Mai, Thailand, she took us to an elephant show where we saw the elephants draw beautiful roses and write the words "Thank you." Another elephant wrote, "I love you." They played basketball and kicked a football between two posts. In a tiger zoo, we watched small tigers being fed milk with a bottle on the laps of my two grandsons. We saw lions and big tigers, which didn't hurt the stewards taking care of them.

We should provide a safeguard to our streams, rivers, and oceans by cleaning and protecting them from pollution. Prevent forest fires in order to save trees and animals and look for other ways to protect the environment. If we don't protect our environment such as the spillage of dioxin and other poisonous chemicals, we will suffer the poisons including the death of living creatures around us.

Last, and most important, is your relationship with Jesus Christ, God's Son. One can strengthen his or her relationship with God by faithfully abiding by His laws, commandments, and teachings. Remember what the first and greatest commandment says: *Love God with all your heart, with all your mind, and with all your soul and with all your strength.*" (Mark 13:30-31) This commandment is repeated in Matthew 22:37-38, Luke 10:27, and Deuteronomy 6: 5.

It is very important that we communicate with God frequently through prayer. We must ask for forgiveness and we must find ways to serve Him, not just ask for favors all the time. If we ask Him what we can do for Him or how we can serve Him, perhaps our prayers will be answered more often because He will direct our thoughts in ways where we can solve our own problems. This has been my personal experience. Loving and serving God should be our priority because He is our total source, including wisdom, good health, peace, happiness, and prosperity.

As a matter of fact, all of the books of the Bible from Genesis to Revelation are about mankind's relationship with God and His creation. The Bible reveals that God is in control of all events, wonderful or catastrophic. God works through the history of mankind in the rise and fall of all empires and their leaders.

Chapter 6
What Successful People Have

1. Successful people have faith and confidence in themselves. They are diligent, industrious, and strive for excellence.
2. Successful people are intuitive, innovative, and creative. They know their weaknesses, but they persevere and maintain a positive attitude until the problem is solved. They know that success is not attained suddenly but by a strong will and persistent effort.
3. Successful people are willing to face challenges and, if they fail, they keep trying again and again.
4. Successful people don't procrastinate. They make thorough evaluations before they make final decisions. They use their time wisely and efficiently. They don't waste time on failure, but use it for learning and problem solving.
5. Successful people maintain good moral attitudes and integrity, which are foundations for righteousness and truth.
6. Successful people eat healthy food and exercise regularly to maintain optimum weight. They realize that diet and exercise are necessary to maintain a healthy heart, mind, body and soul, which may influence their decisions.
7. Successful people are friendly, helpful, kind, and cooperative. They believe in teamwork and understand the acronym: "Together, Everyone Achieves More."
8. Successful people are humble, never arrogant or boastful. They listen to constructive advice.

9. Successful people are full of energy and zest. They laugh and smile often, and have a good sense of humor.

10. Successful people have excellent foresight. They focus on the realization of their goals. Like artists or architects, they mentally visualize the outcome of their goals, which strengthens their enthusiasm and passion.

11. Successful people are optimistic. They study and emulate what inspires them.

12. Successful people have an "I can" attitude. The word "failure" is not in their vocabulary.

13. Successful people become excited when their friends and family members succeed in their own goals.

14. Successful people are honest, trustworthy, and dependable. They know that these attributes build excellent relationships.

15. Successful people are usually less stressed because they are enthusiastic and enjoy what they do.

16. Successful people practice gratitude. They show their gratitude through gifts of appreciation.

17. Successful people know how, when, and where to get help. They aren't afraid to ask: for help during their journey toward success.

18. Successful people prioritize their goals and schedules. They always balance their lives.

19. Successful people listen well to professionals, such as teachers and colleagues. They listen to people with problems so that they may be able to extend help.

20. Successful people learn from other's mistakes, as well as from their own. They may never repeat the same solution, but look for thorough and well-evaluated options.

21. Successful people have a clear, written mission and inspire their company for continued improvement.

22. Successful people make a commitment to the realization of their goals. They are doers and performers more than talkers, because they believe that actions speak louder than words.

23. Above all, successful people honor the Almighty Lord as their leader because they believe that God is their Creator and the source of wisdom, wealth, and other perfect blessings.

Chapter 7
The Fastest and Shortest Road to Failure

It has been said that our altitude is determined by our attitude. Obviously, the many aspects of our lives are determined and dependent upon our responses to the influences of our environment, people, our habits, and, consequently, our character and decision making. While our education is meant to foster our knowledge and understanding of various subjects and, thereby, improve the quality of our lives, it doesn't necessarily bring lasting joy and peace in our lives.

For instance, God created the Universe with its fullness and with all the splendor of its beauty and wealth. There are few people who are in tune to the melodies of nature. Fewer still do not follow the will and teachings of God written for us in the Bible. Consequently, human attitudes are different from one another. Some have great achievement, and some remain miserable and ignorant because they refuse or don't care to enlighten themselves. There are people who are between achievers and failures, who are reasonably content, and never pursue the pinnacle of their dreams.

Perhaps we should assess ourselves more often. Curiosity is needed to ask various questions such as, "Why do we exist?" "What is the purpose of our lives?" "Who or what is responsible for the many good things that we have and enjoy; such as good health, wealth, and peace?" Unfortunately, many countries do not have peace because their leaders are eager for power and want to enrich themselves at the sacrifice of the ordinary people. As a result, poverty increases, which leads to various crimes such as murder, robbery or theft. They also suffer sickness of various kinds leading to death.

Many people do not realize that human beings were created by God to be over and above all other creatures. It is our responsibility to govern or protect them from dangers, which may eliminate their species. Many of us do not realize or exercise the great potential, intelligence, and ability that God has bestowed upon us. We do not realize that there is a living Spirit that dwells within us that can help us do many good things that glorify our Creator and bring true and lasting beauty.

Indeed, there are many questions to which we do not have answers, but if we relentlessly pursue excellence, I believe we can climb to a higher level that leads to a better life. There are those who have achieved many great things in their lives, and have generously shared their secrets through inspiring books. The Bible teaches us the various ways by which we can achieve true success and lasting joy-even eternal heavenly life. So, what are the factors that are responsible for incessant failures?

Procrastination. This is a habit that constantly postpones what needs to be done. The procrastinator always thinks of completing the activity or job tomorrow and never attempts to begin. To reach one's destiny; one has to complete several steps until they reach their targeted destination. Taking action and working toward the fulfillment of one's written goal is the determinant of whether one will succeed.

A poor, young man wants to be rich by the time he reaches the retirement age of sixty-five. He saves 10 percent of his meager salary twice a month and when he has enough money; he invests it in a company that yields high dividends. It is then, automatically; reinvested to buy more shares.

A procrastinator, on the other hand, receives a comfortable check, enjoys life, and buys many unnecessary luxury items, which he cannot possibly use. He thinks that he will have enough money to retire.

Guess who has the most money upon retirement? That's right-the once poor, young man has now become the subject of envy of the rich procrastinator. He now drives a better car and has a better home.

Fear. One of the strongest barriers to success is anxiety. Examples of fear include distress over financial investments and a lack of self-confidence. On the other hand, people with indomitable courage are the winners and achieve success. They love challenges because they know that every problem has its own benefits and solution. They know that there is no barrier to achieving a well-defined goal that is commensurate to their talents. They know that there is an invisible power available to help them if they persist and continue to have positive thoughts.

Lack of Preparation and Resources. No matter how ambitious a person may be, if they do not have the proper training and education, they may not succeed at all. They may be anxious to start their business or project, but in the middle of the journey when problems arise, they don't know what to do or where to turn. They should seek the counsel of experts, take part in a business partnership, or make sure that they properly educate themselves to safeguard against any future problems. Preparation means to educate one's self, not only about business, but to establish good relationships and to improve one's self to be a better, well-rounded, educated individual.

Indecision. Some people are unable to make decisions. Usually, the minds of indecisive people are confused or full of doubts. They cannot focus and fail to arrive at a conclusive and favorable decision. "To be or not to be," is always the question harbored in their minds. Even if the majority of their helpers think otherwise, they still cannot decide to pursue that which they originally planned to accomplish.

Lack of Faith and Enthusiasm. Faith in one's self always generates enthusiasm, and enthusiasm generates hope, passion, and action. A lack of faith quells determination, which prevents one from making commitments, leading to the status quo, or even deterioration. It is through faith that one overcomes barriers and untold adversities. Faith enables one to achieve seemingly impossible goals. It is faith that empowers one to move forward regardless of circumstances that arise. It is faith that makes one perform tasks that must be completed to follow through on commitments.

Lack of Defined, Specified Goals. Sometimes, plans are not executed because the different stages of a goal are not written down or specified. Goals should be clearly defined, prioritized by stage, and measured with a timeframe for accomplishment. By building a timeframe for each step, one can determine the approximate duration of time it will take for the goal to be achieved, find solutions for anticipated problems, and be flexible in case unforeseen problems arise.

Working toward unspecified goals can be likened to a lost person who refuses to stop and asks for directions. Write down your goals so you know exactly what you're working toward. It is like going to a place you have never been before. You should study the map and all the routes in detail and follow through so that you will not get lost; otherwise, you may never reach your destiny.

Negative Thoughts. This is one of the biggest mistakes people make. Negative thinking makes one shut the many doors opened for opportunity. We are made of our thoughts, and even biological reactions in our bodies follow the trends in our thinking. The thoughts on which we dwell determine our moods, emotions, actions, and words. Thoughts are powerful. The thoughts we entertain are what we become. If we think failure, then we are going to fail. If we think positively, then we have a better chance of actually succeeding. We should dwell on positive thoughts constantly, thinking of what is beautiful, noble, and commendable. We should think about problems and their solutions, knowing that problems have their benefits and rewards.

Positive thinking is a mysterious power that floods the mind with creative solutions to existing problems. A negative thought is just like a dark room where no one can see the treasures inside, while a positive thought is like a lighted room where you see all the different treasures, which magnify your desire to achieve.

Lack of Perseverance. This is a poor attitude responsible for failure. Successful people, such as Olympic medalists, persevere until they reach their highest potential. They have unwavering perseverance. They practice countless hours until they excel. They feel that problems along the way are only temporary tests of endurance. Their confidence, patience, devotion, and dedication are strong and enduring. Some impatient people are narrow-minded and shortsighted. They want to stay comfortable and don't like to exert a lot of energy or make an effort to "go the extra mile," which is how victories are won.

Abraham Lincoln failed several times before becoming president. Thomas Edison didn't find the correct part of an incandescent lamp overnight. NASA engineers persisted in developing a vehicle that reached the moon. They did not do so on their first try. After that, NASA was able to make a vehicle that reached the planet Mars to gather and analyze contents of the soil to see if life existed on that planet.

Poor Self-Discipline and Attitudes. The following negative attributes all contribute to failure: selfishness, disrespect, arrogance, laziness, impatience, hypocrisy, and sarcasm. These poor attitudes will slowly bring you down. When you have these attitudes, no one may want to help you on your journey; and these are the strong barriers in the pursuit of your goal(s).

In 1961, there was a man from Lebanon that worked as my co-intern. He wanted to be a surgeon, but he indulged in social life, in conflict with the necessary discipline. He came home late every night. His tardiness at the hospital was an indicator that he may have been drinking liquor, as well. Because of his lateness, he missed many procedures. Because he never changed his lifestyle, he was dismissed. He went back to Lebanon and I never heard from him again.

I had a friend who was supposed to be my business partner. He was also a carpenter. When he was constructing the commercial building that we were supposed to have, I made an observation. I didn't like the way the foundation of the building was made. I told him that this is not the way we build nice buildings in the Philippines. He said, "This is not the Philippines." I told him that effective that day, I was no longer a partner. We remained good friends but shortly after the building was constructed, he developed a chronic disabling disease, taking a lot of medicine every day and no longer able to do anything. He died five years later. I felt so sad for him and his nice family.

Poor Health. A healthy body needs nutritious elements and we should eat the right foods. Diets high in animal fat, salt, and sugar are the risk factors for high blood pressure, heart attacks, strokes, diabetes, obesity, osteoporosis, and other diseases associated with aging. We should eat fresh fruits and vegetables, exercise, and maintain an ideal weight. Regular doctor visits should be a priority, to ensure that we are in the best of health.

These are the main causes of failures. They are the opposite of those mentioned in the earlier article, *"Timeless Principles in Achieving Success."*

Chapter 8
The Greatest Thoughts and Plans for Every Day

Today, I will start and design a new blueprint for my life, which will help me develop enthusiasm, courage, and strength so that I can have greater power and better opportunities to serve my country and my God. This is why I was created and what I was born to accomplish.

Today, I will sit down and carefully assess the causes of my failures and successes in the past. I will find my weaknesses so that they may serve as the source of my strength. May my errors be the source to learn better; may my indiscretions and disgraceful decisions give me the courage to be more humble, prudent, and forgiving. I will consider my failures as my inspirations rather than desperations.

Today, I will learn something new and complete good deeds, so that I may have something to share with my family and friends. I will budget my time properly and wisely, so that I can have enough time for every worthy activity and will be able to achieve the greatest efficiency in all my duties and responsibilities. I will live today as if it were my last, counting every hour as the most precious moments of my life, so that I may accomplish what is worthy, but I will always look to tomorrow for a more challenging, brighter, and greater day.

Today, I will radiate to others the many good things within me. I will be humble and treat all people from all walks of life as special and as the most important people I will ever meet. I will be cheerful and pleasant to everyone. I will be patient and understanding to those who have stubbornly erred. And above all, I will be kind, helpful, and sympathetic to those who need help, hope, faith, and strength.

Today, I will sit and reminisce over my childhood memories. I will think of the days when my mother held me in her loving arms and sang to me melodious lullabies. I will think of the happy years when I played with my brothers and sisters. I will think of the days when my father, whether rain or shine, took me to church to sing songs of praises for the Lord and to hear the minister teach us about the Almighty God!

Today, I will sit down with my family, especially my growing children, and I will teach them how to overcome adversity. I will teach them and reveal to them the arts and secrets of success by inculcating in them the miracles of love, enthusiasm, persistence, and patience. I will emphasize to them the dignity of labor, the crowning rewards of honesty; and the many good blessings and happiness that will enrich their lives by practicing compassion and performing kind acts to others.

Today, I will discipline my whole life to exercise moderation and prudence. I will never indulge myself in any physical pleasure that is harmful to my body. I will search and abide by the rules of good, physical health and mental hygiene in order to attain and maintain myself in the best physical and mental health conditions.

Today, I will call on my friends whom I have not spoken to for a long time. I will ask them how they have been during the time in which we had not seen each other. I will tell them how much I have missed their wonderful company. I will update them on the achievements of my children, their families, and share with them the good things I have learned and ask them, likewise.

Today, I will set a special time to commune with God. I will attune myself into perfect harmony with the perfect universal Power. I will pray fervently for the world's greatest needs: the forgiveness of sins of all men, and lasting peace through cooperation, love, and understanding for all people and all nations. I will pray for the life of everyone; a life full of abundance and good health.

Today I will give back, this day to the Lord before I retire to sleep with this concluding prayer:

Almighty God:

I thank Thee for all the opportunities and blessings You have given me. Forgive me for all the sins and shortcomings I may have and those of my family and friends.

Keep me in Thy strong and loving hands, that I may be shielded from all evil and dangers. Give me strength, wisdom, and good health so that I may be able to work and help Your people. Continue to guide and lead them in the path of righteousness and to fulfill Thy Will.

Above all, may I be worthy to serve Thee. Be my guiding master every moment of my life and, as I fall asleep tonight, I give my whole life to Thee!

Chapter 9
Enthusiasm

Enthusiasm makes all the difference in one's life. Enthusiasm to live life for the better propels one to use all of the talents and efforts one can master. Talents exist in each of us at birth, but one may never develop or realize the talents one possesses. For example, if a teenage boy is exposed to a musical instrument like a violin or guitar, then he can be inspired to take lessons on how to play that instrument. With training, the young man will be able to play simple melodies. His fascination may lead to enthusiasm, and the student's enthusiasm drives him to practice more often. With sustained enthusiasm, eventually, he can master the ability to play the instrument and become a well-known professional.

Enthusiasm kindles a desire to pursue that which one desires to accomplish or become. The intensity of one's desire is directly proportional to the amount and rate of effort exerted. If the enthusiasm is weak, then a goal may take a longer time to be accomplished.

One way to enhance enthusiasm is to set a timeframe for the goal to be accomplished. Setting a timeframe and making a commitment eliminates procrastination and encourages one to work harder. It encourages research in order to develop more efficient strategies. Having a mentor who is familiar with your goal will be beneficial, if not necessary. For instance, I play the violin. However, I could never play like a professional because I have not taken any lessons. If I had been taught basic skills by a teacher, I am sure I would be able to play better.

Enthusiasm is the dynamic force that stimulates your passion to act in the pursuit of your goal. It also strengthens your devotion and persistence in achieving the very best that you can. A marathon runner runs everyday which increases his skill and strength as he continues to train.

Persistence is not making the same mistake, but practicing a different approach that best solves the problem. Indeed, enthusiasm may be defined in an acronym:

E Energy is the dynamic force in the relentless pursuit of excellence.

N Never delay what you can do today because it is a golden moment that should not be wasted. When today is gone, all of the opportunities and joys available will also be gone. Tomorrow will herald its own events.

T Take charge of your life and don't listen to negative comments. In other words, be cautiously active and do your best in whatever you do.

H Homework is very important. Review the stages of your plan and develop strategies to solve specific problems.

U Understand the goal and its different stages, translating it into simple and clear objectives.

S Spiritual force is powerful. With the help of God, nothing is impossible.

I Inspirational attitudes propel one to act upon his/her goal. Ignore hassles and inconveniences, and never let anyone make you turn around.

A Attitudes of determination and perseverance overcome all barriers and adversities to reach your goal.

S Set your goals and plans in such a way that echo your priorities. When you are excited about and enjoy working on your project, there is less room for stress or worry. It also strengthens your faith and determination for success.

M Make your goals and plans come to fruition in a timely manner. Setting a timeframe is a most helpful tip.

Chapter 10
Prescription for Excellence in Teaching Students

In the following, the word "I" refers to the Teacher:

Today, I have discovered the most effective methods to teach my students, so that they can achieve academic excellence and be the very best professionals they choose to be.

I would emphasize and make them realize that they are all born champions and God has given each of them immeasurable talents. They have the ability to explore and develop their talents by constant support and guidance. I would emphasize that the genius within them requires 99 percent perspiration. This means that their intense passion to become the best among the best must be propelled by hard work, intense practice, unwavering perseverance, and tireless dedication. On the other hand, laziness and procrastination are hallmarks of underachievers; that is, people who are content to barely get by. By observing their efforts, I could determine what subjects the students dislike and their reasons.

When I was a student, there was a teacher who evaluated the students based on their habits: why they didn't like the subject, whether they performed assignments or not, and how they used their time at home. This teacher was in a better position to give advice and extend more supervision to explain the subject.

When necessary, teachers should call their students' homes to speak to their parents or siblings to learn how their students spend their free time. Or, better yet, during a Parent-Teacher's Conference, plan ways that could help the students learn more effectively!. I would emphasize to the parents that their contribution, input, and help are very important. They must begin the process to teach children when they are still young. It provides the basis upon which one can be productive.

Good moral conduct and the difference between right and wrong, teach a standard by which decisions are made. Children should be taught to obey their parents, respect others, to be friendly, industrious, honest, and studious. They should also be taught to pray and love God. Children should be taught not to lie, steal, quarrel, use bad language, criticize, boast, or take harmful drugs.

Children learn what they observe in their homes. If a child sees a parent cursing, the child will learn that cursing is permissible. The earliest years are the years during which a child can be easily programmed in the direction of their thinking, attitudes, habits, and character. A good pre-school education will provide a solid foundation for excellence in higher education. Continued support and guidance are extremely important

Once I discovered the problems facing my students, I would find appropriate and specific solutions to address their predicaments aggressively, If the cause were poor understanding of a school subject, then I would spend more time explaining and simplifying the subject in question so that the students can understand and be motivated. If the problem were caused by a student's lack of ability or unwillingness to use his time wisely, then I would urge parents to institute proper disciplinary actions on their child. I would urge them to reform their child's lazy habits to habits that are more productive.

If students do not have adequate materials to read, study; and learn at home, or if their home environment were not ideal for learning, then I would strongly recommend that the students go to a nearby library where they may study.

Every morning before I began to teach a lesson, I would give the students a five-minute quiz. Then, I would ask them to exchange test papers with classmates to review their answers. I would then ask their scores. By doing this, I would be able to tell which students did their assignments and which ones did not. By giving the five-minute quiz, I would motivate the students into studying and performing their best on assignments. For the students who repeatedly make low scores, I would offer my help to instruct them to study better.

I would make an effort every day for my students to never be afraid or ashamed to tell me their problems, so that I may help them in the best way possible.

I would make our classroom a hall of friendship, always motivating and inspiring them so that everyone feels free to help one another.

I would emphasize that discipline, perseverance, continual learning, and practice are the foundations for excellence, both academic and non-academic.

I would teach students the three Rs, or what is required of them in the curriculum for each grade level. I would especially emphasize how to concentrate and focus as they read, so that they might understand more material. After they read an article or story, they should be able to answer the questions, "Who? What? Where? When? Why? How?" When they do this frequently, it would become a positive habit.

When I was in medical school, our assignments were very long and it was almost impossible to remember everything you read. I discovered a technique that enabled me to learn faster without the need to write an outline. I bought a tape recorder, dictated the important parts of the subject that I needed to know. Then, I played the tape before I went to sleep. If necessary I played it again before I got up in the morning. This method enabled me to almost memorize everything that was recorded.

I would teach my students how to think and use their minds by giving them simple puzzles, and then progress with more difficult puzzles as their abilities improved. In other words, I would stimulate their minds for creative thinking and simple problem solving. By doing this, they would be able to overcome adversities and find it easier to solve problems in the future. I would teach and emphasize good moral values such as honesty, humility, respect, cooperation, and generosity which are the crowning virtues on the road to prominence, leadership, and success.

I would encourage my students to join clubs and organizations that interest them, such as 4-H Club or Scouts. If desired, they should also play a musical instrument, play a sport, or meet regularly with a tutor in order to receive a more well-rounded education.

I would teach them about proper nutrition, as well as exercise, so that they may stay healthy and be in better shape to learn. I would encourage them to visit their doctor on a routine basis for a physical and mental check-up, as well as the need for vaccines to prevent diseases.

Finally, I would encourage them to attend their church, to participate in Bible studies, and other activities. I would encourage them to commune with God often in order to strengthen their faith and obedience to His laws and commandments. I would emphasize this because God is the source of wisdom, good health, happiness, and success.

Chapter 11
How a Student May Excel in Academics

Today is the best day of my life. I have discovered the right path to excellence in all endeavors. I am no longer content with myself as an ordinary student, for that status does not lead me to the best school where I can best develop my talent. I realize that my pre-school education is one of the most significant and greatest foundations of good education. I say this because my parents and my elders, aside from books, are my best teachers. They taught me everything they know, and still, they continue to guide and support me.

During my pre-school years, I was molded and programmed to always think positive, to believe that every problem has a solution, that all goals can be reached, and that I can be successful in any profession of my choosing. I was also taught the basic principles of success such as hard work, patience, perseverance, honesty', compassion, cooperation, thoughtfulness, and other good moral virtues and values.

I have read many motivational books such as Think and Grow Rich and the Laws of Success by Napoleon Hill; Success System That Never Fails by William Clement Stone; The Greatest Salesman by Og Mandino and his other books; series of books by Anthony Robbins; and many other inspirational audiotapes produced by Nightingale-Conant. These books created in me a new perspective about life and success. It's as if my eyes were opened wider to see the many opportunities I had never seen or knew before. I encourage everyone to read these books. They seem to give the reader the power to achieve one's heart's desire.

Of course, the Bible is the greatest book of all, because it contains the greatest treasures of life. It is the best map of the road to true success.

As a teenager, I realized that we are created in the image of God, and we are endowed with immeasurable talents beyond our comprehension. God gave us the authority to govern, to be stewards of all living creatures on the earth. Yet, most people are content with using only 5-10 percent of their brains. They are unaware that they have the potential to improve their quality of life.

So, how can we improve the use of our brains to 90 percent or higher? It is said that to be a genius, one must have an IQ of 145 or higher. Some also say that genius is 99 percent perspiration. I am more inclined to believe that the latter is true. Many Olympic athletes and musicians such as Mary Lou Retton, Michael Jordan, Michelle Kwan, Mozart, and even Mr. and Mrs. Snider were not born geniuses. They made frequent mistakes at the beginning, but they were motivated and practiced tirelessly and persistently for years until they became their very best.

Even the discovery of medicines takes years, sometimes even decades, because of the trial and error involved in developing prescription drugs that are safe.

During my high school years and in college, I had the opportunity to observe many students who excelled in academics. I asked them what made them so smart. The reply was almost consistent. They had the passion to be better than anyone else. They worked very, very hard until they became the best they could be.

There was someone I knew who was not getting high grades. Some of his friends became scholars. He thought he was as smart as they were. This motivated him and he promised himself he would prove it. He studied harder and sure enough, he eventually got better grades than the scholars.

So, to excel in academics and other activities, you have to change your beliefs and develop strong faith. You have to have a strong faith, strong enough to withstand obstacles. With the help of God, everything and anything is possible. He has given us the freedom of choice and as long as we don't violate His laws, whatever you conceive can be achieved. This, of course, requires proper discipline, enormous patience, and hard work. Today, we can get almost any information we need so that we may learn more by using the Internet through the computer.

To be the best student you can be, always go the extra mile; meaning, read other books related to your school subjects. In every topic, there are several questions not easily perceived, but which can always be unveiled and answered. You should:

1. Always be punctual in attending your classes and be a model student.
2. Always be enthusiastic, humble, helpful, and friendly because these are the keys to leadership.
3. Always be patient and understanding.
4. Always be resourceful and always search for ways to improve.
5. Always anticipate common failures, so you may work to correct or prevent them.
6. Always seek advice and counsel from experts in order to avoid costly mistakes.
7. Always encourage and praise others and never criticize anyone, for they too have the potential to become better and great.
8. Always encourage cooperation and teamwork, because it allows for achieving more.

To sustain such enthusiasm and intense desire to excel, strength and good health are required. Therefore, take good care of your body. Eat foods with the best nutrition for health, including fruits, vegetables, fiber, meats, low or unsaturated fats, and take vitamins and mineral supplements. If necessary keep your body clean and prevent contamination from transmissible diseases. If you are past the age of forty-five, consult your physician for advice on hormone replacement. Exercise regularly to maintain the tone of muscles to burn excess fat and calories, prevent osteoporosis, maintain an ideal weight, and improve your cardiovascular and pulmonary systems.

You should avoid the risk factors for stroke, heart attack, and cancer by not smoking, not overdrinking alcoholic beverages, controlling diabetes and hypertension, avoiding junk foods, and drinking plenty of water. Make sure to get adequate sleep to rejuvenate emotional, mental, and physical vigor and vivacity.

Always maintain a good attitude and habits and never allow your temper and anger to explode. Take all the vaccinations necessary for the prevention of preventable diseases. Lastly, visit your physician regularly for a thorough checkup and health education.

Nutrition for the mind and the spirit is very important. What are the foods for the mind? First of all, we should differentiate the mind from the brain. It is true that the mind is the function of the brain, and therefore, it is nice to know what foods are good for the brain. Foods that are rich with multiple vitamins are essentially good for the brain. The vitamin B complex is very useful such as B 1 or thiamin, B6 (pyridoxine), folic acid, and B12; also fish oil, lipoic acid, vitamin E complex, vitamin C ester, and many super anti-oxidants. Fresh fruits are excellent foods for the brain such as blueberries, blackberries, cranberries, raspberries, and oranges.

The mind and the spirit are closely related. We should feed the mind with many inspirational books. There are many books on the market today that deal with success, and solving problems and worries. There are medical books that deal with depression, anxiety and many other physical and mental problems. They are written for laypeople without using complicated medical or technical terms.

The contents in the Bible are perhaps the best nutrition for the spirit. There are many hidden treasures, teachings, and inspirational topics that lead to a successful life, peace, and joy. Review the Ten Commandments in the first few pages of this book. Prayer or communication with God is very important. Searching His laws and teachings, having a strong faith, and abiding by His laws and teachings are the keys to achieving the best that you can be. Review also the Be-Attitudes of the high achiever and great leader.

Chapter 12
The Making of a Good Doctor

Becoming a doctor is very challenging. It is difficult, in part, for the length of years to study-four years of undergraduate, four years in medical school, and another four years of residency training. If extra training is needed for a particular field of special like thoracic and cardiovascular surgery; two additional years is necessary. Overall, it took me sixteen years of post-graduate education before I went to private practice.

Medical education and training is a very expensive investment. It requires unwavering patience, incredible passion, and talent. After four years of undergraduate education, one is not sure whether he or she is accepted into medical school. This is so because there are three or four times more applicants than what the college of medicine can accept. Many applicants do not meet the requirements because of insufficient grades, traits revealed during the interview, or lack of focus in extracurricular activities during one's undergraduate years.

After four years of residency, other questions arise as to where you will practice. Should you join a group practice? If you decide to practice on your own, do you have the means to acquire the facilities and equipment to practice? How much is that worth? Can you afford to pay for malpractice insurance? Will you be able to pay the office expenses since Medicare, Medicaid, and insurances have limited reimbursements? These are the costs one should estimate before going into private practice. The best option these days is to be employed by a hospital, which practically pays for one's overhead expenses.

Other factors contribute to how one may be successful to practice his/her profession. During my residency, I observed my professors and attending staff. I noticed some were busy while others had very few patients. I made rounds with them and told them what I had done for our patients.

I concluded that successful practices were based on good relationships with patients. I believe the greatest virtue of a successful practice is the way the doctor establishes his/her relationship with a patient. A good doctor takes his/her time to examine the patient thoroughly. The patient's illness must be explained, how it may have been prevented, and the best known cure. Of course, there is no guarantee for complete healing and one should make it a point that if the patient's health doesn't improve or the medicine doesn't help, the doctor should be notified.

The patient should return as soon as possible for another visit and further evaluation. The doctor should always be honest, friendly, and gentle. One should impart the impression that you really care. o I have a friend who, each time he saw one of his patients, didn't only ask about the patient's condition but also the entire family. He took his time as if that patient was the only patient he had. All his patients loved him and told all of their friends what a wonderful doctor he was. That doctor is now retired. Over the years, I made an outline as to what virtues make "THE GREAT DOCTOR." Here is what I have discovered:

T   **Trustworthy.** A good provider must be trusted, dependable, and faithful to their patients and profession.

H   **Honest.** A physician must be honest and sincere in order for their patients to gain confidence.

E   **Enthusiastic.** Doctors must show a warm interest in helping a patient, whatever problems he or she might have.

G   **Generous and Gentle.** Doctors should be gentle and kind to their patients and make them feel that they have their patient's best interests in mind. Their voice should be tender and not rude. Occasional humor is mostly welcome; after all, laughter is the best medicine.

R **Respectful.** Always be respectful and courteous to your patients regardless of their race, sex, and social status.

E **Efficient and Well-Updated through Continuing Education.** The doctor should have other resources and other experts to consult when attending to difficult cases.

A **Attentive.** Always listen carefully to the problems of the patients. Poor attention and an incomplete medical history may lead to misunderstanding, misdiagnosis, discontentment, and disappointment of the patient, especially if the doctor didn't ask what other problems he/she has.

T **Thorough.** Incomplete physical examinations and history are the causes of many misdiagnoses. Thoroughness minimizes the danger of a wrong diagnosis and inappropriate medication.

D **Dedicated.** This requires patience and perseverance in the overall care of a physician's patients, as well as the profession as a whole. Critical patient care requires energy, talent, and devotion in order to heal. Also, motivating and educating patients helps them to have better health.

O **Outstanding.** It is good to be extraordinary in one's chosen field. It is important to be involved in worthwhile community activities such as educating and giving lectures to the public, and volunteering services in activities such as health fairs.

C **Compassionate, Conscientious, Careful, Cooperative, and Competent.** These five attitudes can "make or break" the satisfaction one experiences with their primary care physician. These attitudes are the best way to prevent malpractice suits.

T **Tracking System.** This simply means a routine follow-up with patients. It is a commendable gesture to call and check how the patient is doing a few days after an examination. Otherwise, it may be good to ask the patient to come back for a re-evaluation, if they are not better.

O **Organization.** It is important for doctors to put things in their proper order to eliminate wasted time in locating supplies. Orderliness in a neat and clean office is the first impression the doctor makes to gain the patient's confidence.

R **Resourceful and Responsible.** It is a great responsibility to be a healthcare provider. Doctors deal with sick people on a daily basis. A minor mistake could lead to a terrible outcome. It is a great consolation to a physician to see that their patients get well. It is imperative that a good doctor knows how to execute their plans in a timely manner.

Finally, an active practitioner must spend adequate time to review his/her current cases. Questions to ponder are: Did I do my best? Are there other options? Was there something I didn't write in my post-op orders? Doing this is especially important if the patient is very ill. In the book The Ministry of Healing, the author strongly emphasizes that a doctor must take the Good Lord as his partner, because He is the greatest physician.

Chapter 13
The "Be" Attitudes of a High Achiever and Good Leader

All of these attitudes make a great difference among great leaders:

T   **Thorough.** A good leader is very thorough in the planning and executing of projects. They visualize every stage of a project and set precise timetables for completion.

H   **Honest**. A good leader is always honest and never cheats or lies, but always maintains unquestionable integrity a good leader refuses to tolerate bribery', no matter how enticing the offer.

E   **Efficient.** A good leader is always searching for opportunities to improve their organizational skills and the working conditions of their employees. They are proactive in leading their staff in brainstorming and problem solving. They also set short and long-term goals for improving the quality and quantity of products or services that will make their company profitable.

G   **Generous.** Thoughtfulness and gratitude are hallmarks of excellent leaders. They reward those who excel in their duties, believing this stimulates and inspires them. They also help people whom they know are in need.

R   **Respectful.** Good leaders know the value of respect and respect everyone regardless of social status, race, or sex. They are open-minded to the opinions of other people and evaluate them all to choose the best option for solutions to problems.

E   **Enthusiastic.** A good leader demonstrates a strong interest in the execution of responsibilities. They are optimistic because they know this is integral to the accomplishment of goals.

A   **Amiable.** A good leader is involved and cooperative while participating in community activities. They are friendly to everyone, not only to fellow leaders, but also to the people who look up to them.

T   **Trustworthy.** Because of their honesty, sincerity, dedication, and competence, an exemplary leader is trusted and dependable.

L   **Listen Well.** A good leader is aware of the importance of listening to the people they lead. It is nice to know if the staff and employees are happy and content.

E   **Energize and Empower.** A good leader will energize and empower the staff so that they will continue to be motivated and work hard for the improvement of the company.

A   **Attentive and Available.** A good leader exercises concern over even the simplest of problems and never procrastinates. They make themselves available when their expertise is demanded, regardless of inconvenience.

D   **Dedicated.** Leadership requires patience and tireless perseverance for overall performance.

E   **Educated.** Good leaders require education, which is a lifetime process. It is mandatory to improve one's own life and the effectiveness of their company. A good leader or high achiever sends their staff or continuing education and shares knowledge with their employees so that the company continues to pursue excellence.

R   **Reviews Frequently.** Good leaders review their goals, their accomplishments, any deficiencies, or ways to perform better or become more efficient. Good leaders continue to improve their vision and mission.

Chapter 14
The "Be" Attitudes of Couples

1. Blessed are the couples that maintain their love and affection long after the wedding bells have rung. Their love, like a redwood tree, grows bigger, taller, and stronger as the years go by.
2. Blessed are the couples who maintain their respect, honesty, loyal and dedication for one another at all times.
3. Blessed are the couples who share each other's happiness and fortunes as well as their hardships and worries.
4. Blessed are the couples who settle misunderstandings and disputes not with insults or shouting, but with respect, compassion, and tender words.
5. Blessed are the couples who understand that no matter how large or small a house is, it is the love, peace, and understanding that make it a home.
6. Blessed are the couples who provide their children with continuous love, educational, spiritual, financial, and emotional support, and guidance to make them better citizens for tomorrow's society:
7. Blessed are the couples who love and respect their parents and siblings and are always willing to extend help to them whenever needed.
8. Blessed are the couples who tirelessly dedicate their talents, wisdom, and virtue for the welfare of others and the glory of God.

9. Blessed are the couples who enjoy and treasure the friendship and love of their friends and neighbors.

10. Blessed are the couples who take the Lord Jesus Christ into their lives as their Savior and who faithfully pray for bountiful blessings for themselves and for others.

11. Blessed are the couples who always pray together, attend church together, and faithfully abide by God's Commandments for they will be blessed with good health, peace, happiness, and success.

Chapter 15
Some Mothers Are More Like Angels

When I was a child, I remember my mother and some of the things that she did on a daily basis. However, the most important thing that she did was to pray every morning before she got up and again before she lay down at night. She kneeled, putting her fingers on her rosary beads one after the other until her prayer was finished. It would take her ten to fifteen minutes to do this ritual. I asked her what she was praying for and she told me that whatever we were doing that day; she prayed that God would always be with us so that everything would turn out well.

My mother had many responsibilities like any mother does today. They go to the grocery stores, cook, clean the house, do the laundry, take the children to team or band practices, and pick them up later. They also mow the lawns, weed the gardens, and help gather the harvest.

When children grow older, they share some of the household responsibilities, like washing dishes, making beds, cleaning shoes, and cleaning the house. Those mothers who have extra time engage in other activities such as volunteering in various community projects or joining the women's auxiliary groups working in hospitals, distributing foods and clothes through organizations, joining women's clubs, or leading in scout groups or 4-H clubs. Mothers who were gifted and highly educated would find work consistent with their education or specialty. Some ran for elective political positions, while others created businesses or established great organizations.

Mother Teresa was an example. She built homes for the orphans in India and provided education for them as well. She was not rich, but managed successfully soliciting adequate financial help from various resources, and with God's help, the projects still exist today and are running well.

There are many mothers today in roles such as executives in big business industries, congresswomen, senators, and in some countries, women who serve as presidents or prime ministers.

Below is my outline for the:

"Be" Attitudes of Mothers

Blessed are the mothers, for they are the living angels on Earth who brought their children into life.

Blessed are the mothers, for their love is fashioned after God's enduring love, endless and unfailing, always bringing hope, strength, and happiness.

Blessed are the mothers, who toil night and day to make their house a home and heavenly sanctuary where souls find comfort.

Blessed are the mothers, for they have patience and endurance to mend their children's clothing. They keep laundry clean and put things in their proper place.

Blessed are the mothers, for they run to the grocery store, filling their kitchens with nutritious delicacies.

Blessed are the mothers, who achieved high academic and political careers, for their enthusiastic service to others exceeds their domestic duties.

Blessed are the mothers, whose cheerfulness and kind acts bring sweet smiles, harmony, and joy to their family, friends, and neighbors.

Blessed are the mothers, who think less of themselves, but constantly endeavor to work for the benefit and welfare for their children.

Blessed are the mothers, for the fine virtues and the wonderful things they do, which make life more pleasant and more enjoyable.

Above all, blessed are the mothers, who pray constantly for God's love and guidance, so that they may raise their children in the wisdom of God who keeps their families faithful, peaceful, and health.

Chapter 16
Prescription for Happiness

"I am come that they may have lift and that they may have it more abundantly." (John 10:10)

"A merry heart maketh a cheerful countenance, but by sorrow of the heart the spirit is broken." (Proverbs 15:13)

Happiness is a state of condition brought about by the harmonious blending of the mind, spirit, and emotion. It is just like a musical trio playing three different instruments in a harmonious and perfect synchrony producing a sweet and pleasant melody. It is not self-gratification or physical pleasure. It is not just laughter, a smile, ease, or comfort. It is not just enjoying what you are doing, but it has to be the right choice, which doesn't hurt anybody or violate any laws. Sometimes it is very hard to define because both wealth and poverty have failed to bring happiness. It doesn't cost a penny, yet, it is the most sought after and the greatest goal in life, as well as the greatest feeling and form of satisfaction.

True happiness is deeply rooted in the fertile soil of contentment and is consecrated by sincere effort and by wise understanding and unfaltering patience. It is often felt after many tears or much perspiration. It is molded and perfected by faith, self-discipline, compassion, and noble deeds. Happiness is a great treasure you cannot buy, transfer, or borrow, because it is created within your soul.

To gain happiness, one has to understand one's self by thoroughly analyzing every aspect of one's life. One should be able to eliminate one's undesirable attitudes and bad habits, as well as those evil thoughts harboring in one's mind. One should never dwell on worries or past unfortunate circumstances, for these things have been done and cannot be undone. One can be happy anytime and anywhere, whenever one makes up his/her mind to be happy!

When negative thoughts enter your mind, switch your thoughts to the many blessings you have had in the past. Think about how fortunate you are to have been born in this world. Think of the enormous wealth and beauty of our country, the many freedoms you enjoy, including freedom of speech, freedom of the press, freedom to assemble, freedom to choose your business, freedom to vote or run for public office, and most importantly, the freedom to worship God. Think about the numerous conveniences available to you that are not available in some developing countries such as televisions, washing machines, cell phones, computers, plumbing, electricity, cars, and public transportation that you can use whenever you wish. One can also enjoy beautiful parks, museums, movies, libraries, and many other conveniences. When you dwell on these things, you begin to feel very grateful to God for the many blessings He has provided you! Allow whatever mistakes, shortcomings, or unrighteous acts you have committed to serve as lessons for discipline and prudence, as well as inspiration for creative thinking and problem solving. Think of the many possibilities and opportunities awaiting you now and tomorrow.

Life has many cycles. It has ups and downs and has many roads along its journey. We have to look far beyond what our eyes can see in order to be able to perceive and follow the right road. There are many temptations, signs, and confusing labels in this world, and if we are not careful, we may end up following the wrong direction and suffering great devastation and misery!

Nothing in the Universe is constant. The only constant thing is the change that takes place from moment to moment. Today may be cloudy and chilly; but tomorrow the sun may shine brightly. The roses may bloom and the birds sing in ecstasy. So, take this moment to attune yourself to the beauties that surround you. Bow your head before heaven and express your eternal gratitude to God who provides you with a wonderful day and other opportunities for a better and happier life. Always think positively. Always look forward to a brighter future, and always think of the magnificent and wonderful beauty of the Universe and the enormous, unfailing love that God has for you. Plant the seeds of love and divine wisdom into your heart and mind and let them grow and flourish with kind words and caring hands. Before you know it, you will find yourself teeming with joy and happiness.

To gain happiness, one has to be able to control not only his actions, but also his feelings and thoughts, and blend them into perfect harmony which results in simplicity and contentment. To gain happiness, one has to adhere to the laws of Divine Providence, the Golden Rule, and good moral values, and stay away from temptation and destructive self-gratification. To gain happiness, one must be able to distinguish between right and wrong, correct the wrong, and be able to stand up once he has fallen. He must be able to smile in the midst of pain and crisis. Because of his faith and resourcefulness, he should be able to "convert his scars into stars," as Dr. Robert Schuller has said. He is the famous minister of the Crystal Cathedral Church in Orange Grove, CA. One should understand and affirm that happiness comes after one has overcome many failures and miseries due to faith, confidence, patience, and dedication.

To gain happiness, one must be capable of forgetting one's lost loved ones. Because we are deeply and emotionally attached to those whom we loved and lost, such as a husband or wife, it is natural that we feel lonely and sad. We ought to remember that death is inevitable. Physical life has its beginning and its end. Being lonely is not going to change the physical death. Sometimes, to a patient who suffers constant pain due to incurable illness, death is much preferable than living. Hence, one should comfort one's self because the loved one is no longer living in miserable pain.

To gain happiness, nourish the mind by reading inspirational and motivational books. Learning is a lifelong journey. It should be a commitment in order to adjust and adopt one's self to improving the environment. We should focus and also to learn, and do the things that make life better. This is what our loving God wants us to be and do.

To gain happiness, one has to be able to exercise the freedom to pursue happiness. In past years, in China and Russia, there was no freedom of religion. One was not allowed to practice religion or worship freely. They could not gather together in a church to pray to

God. Thank God, things have now changed. There are missionaries teaching to worship God in hidden temples or churches regardless of their religious sect.

More on happiness as quoted from the notes of Dr. Kind N. Loving Jr.: "Happiness is the joy of sending flowers to a friend or loved one with a card that states, 'Every leaf and petal of these flowers express how much I long to hear from you; how much I long to closely embrace you that you may feel the pulsating love emitting from every beat of my heart.'

"Happiness is something I cannot define. Although I lost my hearing in one ear, I still have the other one to appreciate the melodious songs of birds, the sound of the crickets, the sound of the gentle breeze as the soft wind passes by; and to hear the pulsating sound of the ocean waves.

"Happiness is that sense of gratitude that although I lost the vision of my one eye, I still have one left to appreciate the beauty of a rose, the multi-colored leaves of different trees during autumn, as well as the magnificent and spectacular national parks in USA, and to be able to see the million stars hanging in the heavenly sky.

"Happiness is the sense of gratitude that although I am disabled and paralyzed, I still have a motorized wheelchair to allow me to move around and a loving wife to extend all her loving heart and soul to assist and provide many things that I need.

"Happiness is a sense of joy that, although I have aged, I still remember the many joys of having seen my grandchildren growing healthy, going to church, and learning about God, His teachings, and their fear to deviate from the right path. I still enjoy and understand the evolution of the growing beautiful world, the progress of technology that makes life better in many ways. I still feel and understand the steadfast love of the Almighty God and continue to gain new information, which I can use to inspire others.

"Happiness is a special gift seeing that my children received good educations and are practicing their profession to the best they can be and not forgetting their brother, sisters, and parents, yet inspiring others for the glory of our Creator and Savior.

"Happiness is a joy that evolves from the little things that someone shared, not because of their material value, but by the unmeasured loving thoughtfulness of a faithful and caring friend.

"Happiness is most felt after having lived over a great devastating misery-be it an injury or sickness or the loss of the most loving spouse.

"Happiness is a joy of knowing and seeing the many charitable foundations helping many needy people and other poor countries; the abundance and wealth of this country and the good leaders blessed with wisdom to lead this democratic country.

"Happiness is a joy with tears knowing that the Holy Spirit, which you cannot see, but exists in your mind, stores enormous love in your heart emitting its energy to every fiber of your soul making your life so peaceful, undefined by any words.

"Finally, happiness is the greatest gift and blessing that one has regardless of gender, social status, race, and beliefs, because we have a most loving and forgiving God who is the source of wisdom, good health, peace, and everlasting joy."

Indeed, true and lasting happiness is the result of a healthy mental attitude, grateful spirit, a clear conscience with contentment and satisfaction, and a heart full of love, all of which are perfect blessings from our gracious Almighty God!

In another way of concluding, HAPPINESS stands for:

H   **Healthy** body, mind, and soul.
A   **Active** in various affairs not only to his/her domestic duties or hobbies and profession, but also to some charitable organization.
P   **Peaceful** attitudes leading to a peaceful life.
P   **Prudence and Perseverance** leading to righteousness.
I   **Industrious and Inspired** about living in fullness despite many handicaps.
N   **Noble** in thoughts and in actions leading to integrity.
E   **Enthusiastic** to do everything good.
S   **Sincere** in all her/his motives.
S   **Slow** to anger in what one does

Chapter 17
The Meaning and Power of Faith

Faith is probably best defined in the Book of Hebrew 11:1 *"Now faith is the substance of things hoped for, the evidence of things not seen."* How can faith move mountains or cure illnesses? How is it that faith can transform or make things happen, things that once seemed impossible to do? Was or is Jesus Christ the only person who did the impossible things? Wasn't Peter also able to cure a lot of illnesses during his apostolic time, as found in the Bible in Acts 3:7-9?

A lame man was brought to the gate of the temple to ask for alms every day and Peter said to him, *"Silver and gold have I none; but such as I have give I thee; In the name of Jesus Christ of Nazareth rise up and walk. And he took him by the right handy and lifted him up; and immediately his feet and ankle bones received strength. And he leaping up stood, and walked, and entered with them into the temple, walking, leaping and praising God."*

Perhaps, it was and still is done by our Almighty Creator who causes incredible and seemingly impossible events to happen. As the Bible says: *"Jesus is the same yesterday, today and forever."* He controls the direction of the winds and rains, and establishes all the natural laws of and in the Universe. He still heals and works through His Holy Spirit. How can one achieve or perform such things? If the Apostle Peter could do it, can we do it as well? There must be an explanation. Matthew 17:20 says: *"And Jesus said unto them, 'because of your unbelief for verily I say unto you, If ye have faith as a grain of mustard seed, ye shall say unto this mountain, Remove hence to yonder place, and it shall remove; and nothing shall be impossible unto you."*

Likewise, the Book of Philippians states: *"I can do all things through Christ who strengthens me."* Take a note on the following verses-Matthew 21:22 says: *"And all things, whatsoever ye shall ask in prayer; believing, ye shall receive."* John 14:12-14 says: *"verily, verily, I say unto you, He that believeth on me, the works that I do shall he do also; and greater works than these shall he do; because I go unto my Father. And whatsoever ye shall ask in my name, that will I do, that the Father may be glorified in the Son. If ye shall ask anything in my name, I will do it."*

Pastor Robert Schuller of the Crystal Cathedral in Orange Grove, California, started his ministry in a parking lot, gradually built a large cathedral in California, and extended his ministry to several countries through radio and television. There are other ministers who are/were able to build large churches.

When the late Henry Ford designed the first Model-T car, he told his engineers to make one, which they did because of his strong faith that it could be done. Likewise, Thomas Edition failed a thousand times before he could find the right part for an o incandescent lamp. He didn't quit.

The Bible states: *"Seek ye first the kingdom of God and His righteousness and all these things will be added unto you."* I believe the fundamental issue is to be right with God. To be right with God means to be faithful, obedient, and to follow His teachings. Only when you are in harmony with God are you able to do many seemingly impossible deeds.

I believe that every action that we commit to is based on faith. Faith is also confidence in action and it is the dynamic force that strengthens and enriches hope when everything is gone or lost. It is the mental engine that powers patience and generates enthusiasm, which is the strongest and the greatest foundation of all achievements and successes. It is the spiritual force that perhaps comes only from the power of the Holy Spirit who can do anything because with Him nothing is impossible. Without faith, life becomes worthless and meaningless, and failure or death is the outcome.

I have seen many patients during my years in surgical practice who were critically ill having sustained severe, multiple injuries to the chest and abdomen with extensive loss of blood. They were in shock when they arrived in the emergency room, and if left alone, they would have surely died within a few minutes. However, because we were trained to resuscitate critically injured patients by rapid replacement of blood lost and because we had a team available, many patients survived.

As a Christian, I've learned to define faith by this acrostic:

F   **Fulfillment** of God's will, teachings, and commandments so that one may dwell in harmony and righteousness with Him.

A   **Action,** which is service to God and to others, especially the needy regardless of age, race, sex, religion, or social status. It means aspiring for the eternal life in the promised kingdom of God.

I   **Inspiring** others to work for God and instructing His Gospel throughout the world, so that people may be enlightened and receive His wisdom, which is the greatest treasure of life.

T   **Trusting** and loving the Lord Jesus Christ with all your heart, with all your might and your soul, and without doubt and reservation.

H   **Honoring** God with fervent prayers and with deepest and most sincere gratitude.

Chapter 18
The Power of the Mind and Subconscious Mind

It has been said that we have two minds-the conscious mind and the subconscious mind. The power of the mind has been the topic of many books. The mind is most likely the function of the brain. It cannot be described anatomically, but its functions are infinite and, as such, no one can adequately describe its functions. (Read The Creative Power of the Mind by Willis H. Kinnear.)

God created us in His image. Genesis 1:27 *"So God created man in His own image, in the image of God created he him; male and female created He them."* (KJV)

When we talk about image, we usually refer to physical appearance or in the nature of form. No one has seen God, although God exists in the person of Jesus Christ. (See St. John 1:1,10; 14:9-12.)

When God created mankind, He made us very special and very different from animals. I believe that when God created us in His image, He gave us minds that were similar to His. As long as we are in good harmony or right with Him, the Holy Spirit that dwells in us allows us to perform many wonderful things.

We are given talents and abilities to create wonderful things, which other creatures cannot do. Man has made jet planes and flying rockets that travel faster than sound and are capable of exploring other planets. We have discovered numerous types of energy in our atmosphere with different wavelengths for fast communications. The mind doesn't have eyes, but can create forms visible on the mental screen. It creates thoughts powerful enough to make things happen. It can make music play in the mind before the notes are written, so that the music may be played over and over again. It has enormous mathematical expertise and can solve many difficult problems. The mind is the most powerful sense we possess. I call it the sixth sense. It can analyze both the invisible and visible. It can interpret signs of love, anger, happiness, or worry Above all, the mind can map, scan, filter, and choose the frequency of energies in the quantum world to pick up ideas or intelligence upon which all known and unknown knowledge exists. 1 John 4:4 states: *"Ye are of God, little children and have overcome them, because greater is he that is in you, than he that is in the world."*

Although the mind reflects our intellectual ability, I don't believe that the IQ (intelligent quotient) is necessarily a true measure of the capacity of the mind. I am aware of many people who have average IQs, but excel in many areas that no one could have previously predicted. I am also aware of many students whose IQs are high, yet they remain unsuccessful in their life's adventures.

Some believe that the conscious mind is responsible for activities such as planning and thinking. The subconscious mind on the other hand, is responsible for the creative mechanisms that are built into our body's system generating intuition and ideas that are then relayed to our conscious mind. It works automatically and is responsible for the digestion, oxidation, respiration, detoxification, and many other metabolic, biologic, and chemical changes and reactions taking place in our bodies. It is responsible for filing and recording our thoughts and activities in the appropriate parts of our brain. (Read the Automatic Function of the Subconscious Mind by Anthony Norvell.)

One of the most fascinating activities our minds perform is our self-image, both current and desired. When one persistently; sincerely; and faithfully impresses upon the mind what one desires to be, then the subconscious mind automatically works to produce that outcome. In other words, if one stays mentally focused on their desires, provided one makes positive actions, eventually the desired outcome is realized. Remember what the Bible says: *"As a man thinketh in his heart, so is he."* (Proverbs 23:7)

If we are made up of our own thoughts, then we become what we think. People who are depressed, anxious, and worried may remain in that mood because they always think and feel that way. They dwell on unhappy thoughts. They have negative ideas in their minds and essentially say to themselves, "I don't have the ability and I am always a failure." If they change their thinking to a more positive outlook and keep telling themselves that they are capable, then their subconscious mind helps them to achieve their goals.

The subconscious mind is what everyone uses to create or design new inventions. The late Napoleon Hill and Henry Ford used meditation to invoke their subconscious mind to help them accomplish their goals. I used this method in my design for a vascular bypass catheter and today it is widely used in carotid endarterectomy. The procedure allows blood flow to continue as a surgeon removes arterial plaque and prevents ischemic stroke. I believe the subconscious mind is used by everyone unknowingly in their pursuit for excellence, for inventions, and for alternative solutions to problems.

It has been said that everything that is created in the Universe exists in the form of energy. (Read There is a Spiritual Solution to Every Problem by Dr. Wayne Dyer.)

All of our thoughts and ideas, including those who have gone before us, are all in the form of energy. Also, God and the Holy Spirit exist in the form of energy. Our subconscious mind has the power to access energy of an object, thought, or idea that one wishes to achieve mentally. Knowing this basic principle, one may achieve a goal that seems impossible. We can perform beyond our normal capabilities. Thank God for this revealed wisdom! We can use our subconscious mind for healing our bodies, and for getting rid of our unhealthy habits and thoughts so that we can become a better person.

Chapter 19
The Various Meanings of Discipline

Discipline is the art and science of attitude, whereby energetic thoughts and actions are processed in an orderly fashion that bring about better outcomes. Discipline is what brings life and makes the whole world peaceful. Without discipline, life might become a chaotic devastation and the world might become a filthy and poisonous environment. Every living creature has certain disciplines. All the lowest forms of animals, even the microorganisms, have some form of discipline. The birds and other animals feed their young and protect them from destruction until they are capable of taking care of themselves. Even the planets are disciplined to follow their own orbits so that they will not bump against one another. Without discipline, there would be no rest or peace. Each one becomes self-centered with less compassion for one another. There might be constant aggression, fighting, lolling, and only the strongest and wisest left to survive.

To have discipline means to be more righteous, ethical, and legal. It means to have insight and foresight of your objective. It means to have understanding and comprehension between right and wrong, as well as righteous and evil. It means to have confidence and faith to succeed without making many mistakes or worrying.

To have discipline means to be willing to accept temporary defeat in order to win. It means to be honest, reliable, trustworthy; and dependable, which may lead to righteousness, admiration, integrity;

and success. To have discipline means to be flexible, creative, and resourceful.

To have discipline means to be well organized with a concrete and well-defined plan to achieve your goals. It means to exert a greater effort and to carry a heavier load in order to enhance and acquire greater values. It means to endure a more painful course of action in order to experience a more lasting enjoyment. It means using more eyes, hands, feet, and ears than ordinary. It is just like working in a team.

In summary, discipline is:

- Avoiding the path that leads to destruction.
- It is like walking on a narrow beam, balancing your body so you won't fall.
- It is like swallowing the bitter part before tasting the sweet part.
- It is like starving yourself before feeling well fed.
- It is meeting resistance in order to climb higher.
- It is like frowning before being able to smile.
- It is practicing and failing in order to develop patience, but getting better.
- It is like staying away from the crowd in order to concentrate and focus on reaching your goals.
- It is like eliminating all the dirt (mistakes) making you clean and polished (perfect).
- It is like bending your body before straightening it.
- It is like finding a needle in a haystack.

Discipline maybe summarized in this acrostic:

D   Doing the right thing: studying, analyzing, and then carefully making decisions.

I   Improving one's character, attitudes, and habits in order to gain a better life.

S   Searching and seizing the opportunities to excel

C   Concentrating on the rules of righteousness and success.

I   Involving others to help you achieve a better outcome.

P   Planning well-organized activities and completing them with patience.

L   Living a better and more peaceful life for yourself and others.

I   Having integrity: choosing to do what is lawful, ethical, and socially acceptable.

N   Having nobility: achieving all possible ideals that lead to prominence.

E   Having enthusiasm: an inspirational and vigorous attitude to pursue excellence.

Chapter 20
There Are Better Choices in Life

It is surprising how few people realize that one of the best and the most precious gifts endowed to mankind is his liberty and freedom to choose. Although we are aware of this gift, we don't use it properly. Although we are influenced by various factors and respond according to our perceptions, such responses are not always the best choice. Unfortunately, due to ignorance and constant repetition of one's activity, it becomes a habit whether it is unpleasant, destructive, or disgraceful. Some realize that a change is necessary because they see the damage they have caused.

People who smoke are good examples of this theory. Let's think about an individual who smokes two packs of cigarettes a day. He knows that smoking may cause cancer, emphysema, high blood pressure, a stroke, or a heart attack, but he continues to smoke, causing damage. I know people who have had smoke-related heart attacks, but despite the many warnings from doctors or family members, they still continue to smoke. Those who have developed severe emphysema and are already gasping for breath finally quit smoking hoping their condition will improve. But the fact is, irreversible damage has been done. Their quality of life has diminished considerably. They are now miserable because they require almost continuous use of oxygen and daily medication.

Unfortunately, most of us are programmed to only satisfy the needs and pleasures of our bodies. We do not realize (or we choose to ignore) that some of these temporary pleasures are very harmful to our bodies. Many times, although we know these actions are harmful, we insist on continuing them because they give us a feeling or sense of joy or pleasure. We completely ignore that the future outcomes are so damaging.

God has created mankind higher than the angels, and made us in His image. Genesis 1:26 "*And God said, 'Let us make man in our image, after our likeness; and let them have dominion over the fish of the sea, and over the foul of the air; and over all the cattle and over all the earth, and over all the things that creepeth upon the earth.*" Genesis 1:27 "*So God created man in his own image, in the image of God; male and female created he them.*" He loves us, yet He doesn't restrict us from doing the things we want to do. He gave us brains and intelligent minds so that we can use them to gain a better quality of life. They were meant for us to use judiciously and righteously so that we may live long, healthy lives filled with comfort, peace, and happiness.

We make mistakes and we have a lot of shortcomings, but God is always willing to help us improve ourselves. He gave us a guide to life, the Bible, so that we may learn to not only know Him, but also follow and abide diligently by His instructions. He even sent His Son, Jesus Christ, to teach the people of the world and to die for our sins. He taught us how important it is to love God with all our heart and how, by following His commandments, we may be blessed.

We often ignore our spiritual life, which is the dynamic force that connects us to God. When we ignore our spirituality, we are far from the Holy Spirit of God. We are not on the right path. Instead, we lead ourselves into worlds of misery and failure.

Mankind has many beautiful and better options available. We should choose to educate ourselves to the many simple things that improve our quality of life. We should know the difference between right and wrong, between ethical and unethical, and avoid the latter. We should try to stay healthy by avoiding harmful habits such as smoking or drinking alcohol in excess. Because good health is necessary', we should visit a physician regularly for a thorough checkup, maintain an ideal weight, eat the right foods, and avoid too much sugar, aspartame, trans-fatty acids, and too much animal fat.

We should smile and laugh rather than frown. Happiness secretes endorphins that ease pain, anxiety, fear, and worries. Endorphins are the natural morphine-like substances in the body secreted by the pineal gland. Endorphins are hormones that ease pain or discomfort and help create a sense of wellness.

It is important to practice the fine virtues of mankind such as loving rather than hating, generosity rather than selfishness, dedication rather than procrastination, patience rather than haste, and forgiveness rather than hate.

We should remain open-minded and understanding rather than narrow-minded. We should not refuse to accept or at least evaluate other ideas that there may be better solutions to existing problems.

We should aspire to and pursue excellence and not be content with the status quo. There is always room for improvement.

We should pursue lasting joy and happiness. It is our birthright to be happy because we are born with many blessings from the good Lord. We should not weep or worry because God has provided everything we need on this planet. We can be as happy as we choose. We are made up of our own thoughts and beliefs. Our body and all the chemical reactions taking place in our body respond according to the thoughts we choose to think. Because we can control our thoughts, we can control our reactions and feelings. We should never dwell on the thoughts that make us feel lonely, depressed, hopeless, or worried. Whenever thoughts like these come to mind, we should switch our minds to thoughts of the beautiful and the countless blessings provided for us.

May I remind you that the greatest thing you now have is yourself-born with a body, mind, and spirit capable of making the right decision. You were chosen to be born-one out of several millions sperm cells. You were fertilized by one out of several egg cells from your mother. After that, you survived many obstacles from fertility to birth and from birth to adulthood. You were given a free primary and secondary education and even a free bus ride to go to school. Your parents provided you with love and all the necessities and material possessions until you were able to live on your own.

Think of the many beautiful parks, mountains, lakes, and many plants and animals that thrive in them. Reflect on the beautiful buildings and malls where we work and shop. Think of the many intelligent, kind, loving, and generous people you know. These are just a few good things. There are endless, wonderful creations that surround you for which you should feel blessed.

We should choose to forgive. There is a saying that "to err is human, but to forgive is divine." Ephesians 4:32 *"Be ye kind one to another; tenderhearted, forgiving one another even for God, for Christ's sake hath forgiven you."* No one except Jesus was known to be perfect. That is why we should be very careful of what we say or do in order to minimize errors or hurt one another with our words or actions. As the Bible says, only when you forgive others can you be forgiven. Colossians 3: 13 *"Forbearing one another; and forgiving one another; if any man has a quarrel against any; even as Christ forgives you, so also do ye."* Choose not to criticize or condemn others because if you do, then you are judging yourself and, like a boomerang, the judgment will come back to you.

Lastly, we should choose to believe in God, to love Jesus Christ, and to abide by His commandments, teachings, and precepts, for they are the source of wisdom, life, good health, peace, happiness, and an overall successful life.

I would like to end this chapter with a prayer:

Almighty God: Because You made me a physician, may my thoughts and actions be an instrument of Your healing power. Where there is stress and worry, let there be peace and happiness. If there is fear and doubt, may there be courage and faith. If there is weakness and failure, may there be strength and success. If there is greed and selfishness, may there be generosity and compassion. If there is haste and mistake, may there be patience and prudence. If there is hate and cruelty, may there be love and empathy. If there is darkness and ignorance, may there be light and understanding. If there is sorrow and despair, may there be joy and hope. If there is desperation and disappointment, may there be inspiration and enthusiasm. If there is crime and sin, may there be forgiveness and reformation.

Lord Jesus, I pray that I may be a helper and motivator, and that I would comfort and inspire. I pray that I would be understood and know the truth. It is in helping others that we receive rewards. It is in praying that we are in contact with God. It is in practicing righteousness that we gain honor, and it is by being faithful to God and abiding by His commandments that we love God. It is by His grace that we gain eternal life.

Chapter 21
The Greatest and the Best Things in Life Are Free

There are many beautiful mansions, luxurious palaces, and extravagant vehicles in the world today. There are human-created monuments like the Eiffel Tower in Paris, France, and the Taj Mahal in Agra, India. These are all magnificent and beautiful, but are they the best things in life? While we may call them great, they are extremely expensive, and they required enormous effort to build these huge buildings like the gorgeous and most luxurious hotel recently built in Dubai, which is the tallest building in the world. These buildings, like any other buildings, are subject to change and destruction. In other words, they are not immune to damage from earthquakes, fires, hurricanes, or tornadoes.

What, then, can be more valuable than these? Through what criteria can we call things the best or the greatest, and, yet, cost nothing? I believe that the things which are the best and the greatest are those that provide everlasting joy, peace, and true success. They have immeasurable benefits. So, what are these things? The elements include:

A Healthy Mind. Everyone is born to have a healthy mind except, of course, a few who have genetic and inheritable disease such as Down Syndrome. Others develop Autism and Attention Deficit Hyperactive Disorder. But, acquiring wisdom is a different thing. Proverbs 1:7 says: "*The fear of the Lord is the beginning of knowledge; but fools despise wisdom and instruction.*"

I had friends in school that excelled in academics. They had good grades and they became so arrogant that eventually they lost their best friends. They were unable to find jobs after graduating from college. James 1:5 says: "*If any of you lack wisdom, let him ask of God, that giveth to all men liberally, and upbraideth not; and it shall be given him.*"

When I was in active practice, seriously ill and dying patients came to me as if nothing could be done, as if death was inevitable. I could hardly sleep thinking what else could be done to help them. I prayed and asked God to help me. He seemed to have enlightened me saying, "Go back to the basics." So, I went back to the pathophysiology (causes and explanations for diseases, of the disease. Sometimes, I found the answer and the patient recovered. I could not help but say; "Thank you, Lord, for your help. What a joy to see my patients get well."

When King Solomon assumed the kingship, he asked God for wisdom so that he could rule his people wisely and righteously. God was impressed with his request and, as a bonus, gave him wealth beyond imagination. He built beautiful temples, homes, and many other buildings layered with gold. Many kings and queens visited him and gave him precious and wonderful treasures. He took part in writing the book of Proverbs, I Kings, Ecclesiastes, and the songs of Solomon. These books in the Bible are full of wisdom.

Wisdom is the result of lessons learned from a lifetime of experience. It is the backbone of integrity and courage. It cannot be bought, but it can be acquired through the grace of the Lord. In the Book of John 14:13, Jesus says: "*And whatsoever ye shall ask in my name, that I will do, that the Father may be glorified in the son.*" It appears that Jesus Christ is our middleman to access God. However, there are also verses in the Bible where Jesus Christ is God Himself. These verses are found in the Book of St. John 1:1: "*In the beginning was the WORD and the WORD was God.*" John 1:14 "*and the WORD was made flesh and dwelt among us.*" Also St. John 11:30 "*I and my Father are one.*" Also St. John 11:18 "*That ye may know, and believe that the Father is in me and I in Him.*" John 15:7 says: "*If ye abide in me, and my words abide in you, ye shall ask what ye will, and it shall be done unto you.*"

I firmly believe that God is the very source of wisdom. To gain knowledge is to learn from various teachers and read as many books that deal with the subject in which we are interested. (See the prescription of excellence.)

A Healthy Body. To have a healthy body is to apply the laws of good health. It is important to nourish your body with the best nutrition, to exercise, maintain an ideal weight, to be vaccinated' and to visit your physician regularly. Since I retired fifteen years ago as a private practitioner and five years ago as Certified Medical Director in Long Term Care, I have never stopped learning how to stay healthy. I am fascinated with the importance of proper nutrition, which I now believe that eating the right food is the best preventive and curative medicine. I subscribe to the yearly White Papers from Johns Hopkins, which discuss many various topics, The Harvard Health Letter, The journal of Health and Longevity, The Health Letters published by Dr. James Balch and Dr. Robert J. Rowen, The journal of Integrative Medicine, The Life Extension journal, Bottom Line Medical Breakthrough, The Natural Cure by Dr. Stengler, and Health Alert published by Lombardi Publication. I continue to buy traditional textbooks of medicine such as Current Diagnosis and Treatment and Understanding Pathophysiology. I enjoy reading The Disease Prevention and Treatment published by Life Extension Foundation, Growing Old Without Aging by Dr. Miller also published by Life Extension Foundation, Textbook of Natural Medicine by Pizzarno and Murray; Textbook of Functional Medicine edited by David Jones, and Clinical Guidelines in Family Practice. My voluntary membership with the West Virginia University Cancer Control and Prevention through the Mountain of Hope has provided me additional learning experiences.

I receive the monogram on the latest management of various cancers, and participate actively in many teleconferences sponsored by Cancer Care. I have numerous references about complementary medicine, PDR on Herbal Medicine, Nutritional Biochemistry, The Creative Power of the Mind by Willis H. Kinnear, The System That Never Fails: the Science of Success Principles by William Clement Stone, The Power of Positive Thinking by Dr. Norman Vincent Peale, and books by Dr. Nicholas Perricone. I feel like I know more about diseases and their management now than when I was in active practice. I have learned a lot about the true wonders of various supplements, which prescribed medicines cannot provide.

Love. Love is the greatest thing in the world. Everything is created and founded upon love. We are created to love and be loved. Without love, nothing can exist. Love is the force that links and connects all living creatures in harmony, peace, and joy. Because God is love, there is nothing that love cannot accomplish. Even the most ferocious enemy or animal can be tamed and subdued. You cannot buy love just as you cannot buy happiness, because it is intangible. It is free and it is created from within us, but it can be expressed in many ways.

If you have love, God dwells in you, because God is love. If true love dwells within you, there is no worry, no fear, no anxiety, no hate, anger, darkness, or loneliness. Instead, pure and true love makes our lives beautiful, peaceful, joy-filled, and happy; which are the essences of true and ultimate success.

Faith. It is the substance of things unseen. It is the invisible force that strengthens hope. Without faith, there is no progress and everything stands still or deteriorates. Faith is the spiritual power that connects us to God's universal power so as to activate our best dormant desires. Faith powers enthusiasm so that we can accomplish our goals. Faith is the willpower that helps anyone believe that they can become what they wish. It is the magical and spiritual force that heals any illness. It is the invisible force that helps one attain the seemingly impossible. Absolute faith in God, Jesus Christ, one's self, and others yields beautiful and successful outcomes. (Read "The Power of Faith" article elsewhere in this book.)

Prayer. Prayer or meditation is one method of communicating to our Creator, God, His Son, Jesus Christ, and the Holy Spirit. Deep prayer or meditation is communing with God. It is not only talking to Him, but it is being with Him and Him being with you. It is the most blissful relationship anyone can experience. With Him and in Him, we feel indescribable peace that passes all understanding. We can perform great and mighty things, which we once thought to be impossible. We acquire knowledge and wisdom that we never had, we can influence others to make our environment a better place in which to live and, above all, we can discover and feel a sense of true joy and happiness. To pray costs us nothing but the willingness to sincerely talk to Almighty God.

Gratitude. This is the expression of appreciation for a favor shared by someone. Saying "thank you" to someone who has done a favor or service to you implies several connotations between the giver and the receiver. It is not just a casual expression. It has a powerful impact upon the recipient. For instance, if you saw a car accident and helped rescue the driver from the car and called an ambulance, he would most likely be extremely grateful for your help. It would mostly create in you a sense of heroism and gratefulness to God for the ability to have done such a service. This is free and a very commendable effort. This will glorify God and He will bless you in many other ways. This is fulfilling the second law of God, "Love thy neighbor as thyself."

Gratitude or gratefulness denotes a sense of appreciation for a rendered service or favor, and for many opportunities available that may be experienced to make life better, more comfortable, peaceful, and joyful.

Cheerfulness. A smiling face is not only a sign of cheerfulness, but it is an expression of the pleasant behavior and attitude of your inner-self, which is the real you. Smiling is an attitude of happiness, a sensation of well being. It can initiate the secretion of endorphins, which may relieve stress, anxiety; and pain. That is why psychologists say; "Laughter is the best medicine." Laughter is powerfully contagious. Just take a look at the popularity of the Jay Leno Show and the David Letterman Show. Not only do they entertain their studio audiences, but television viewers as well. It's no wonder that comedy shows are so popular!

The Virtue of Industry, Dedication, and Perseverance. Industry, dedication, and perseverance are foundations for success and prosperity. A lazy man, no matter how rich he is, may eventually lose his wealth. Though he may have ambitions, if he lacks dedication and a willingness to persevere, he will never be able to achieve his goals. Hard work and untiring perseverance are the greatest weapons to overcome all adversities. They are like spiritual forces that propel you forward to attain your goal or destiny.

I knew a LPN (License Practical Nurse) in Roane General Hospital who wanted to be a doctor. She was in her late thirties and a single mother. She would work double shifts on weekends to support herself and her daughter. After she finished her premed requirements, she got a student loan for her expenses into medical school. She went on to get her residency in emergency medicine, and then, finally, was able to become a board certified emergency doctor. Her success was the result of her dedication and perseverance.

Amiable and Friendly. These are important traits because they are the elements of humility and accessibility. Some of the greatest leaders such as Abraham Lincoln, former Philippine President Ramon Magsaysay and even Jesus Christ, possessed these traits. If you are unfriendly, selfish, and arrogant people not only dislike you, but also they lose their respect and honor for you. You will end up losing your friends, become isolated, lonely and unwanted by the people of your community. Good attitudes are free. They bring not only joy to one's self but also to others.

Prudence and Righteousness. Prudence is a step towards righteousness, and righteousness is the foundation of truthfulness, which is the essence of good moral character and integrity. Truthfulness erases doubts, lies, fears, and pretensions. Without righteousness and truthfulness, all things become useless and everything loses its value. When there is no righteousness, the world becomes a turbulent, chaotic, and dangerous place to live. Life becomes meaningless. Without prudence, everything may lead to failure.

In the years 2000 and 2001, many investors lost their fortunes. Today some are still losing their small investments. For some it was because they followed television advertisements. They did not investigate whether the company had good products or good financial histories. They did not know if competent and honest leaders managed the companies. Some companies went bankrupt. They issued false statements saying that their income was great, and that they expected to increase their sales and income. What happened? Their CEOs lied and their clients lost their money. Truly, prudence is a great thing to have to avoid costly mistakes.

Obedience. A child's obedience to his/her parents creates a wonderful relationship. Obedience to your superior is like the military; it establishes good discipline. Obedience to your boss, parents, or elders also denotes respect. In competitive games, obedience to a good coach assures a better chance of winning. Obedience to laws creates peaceful societies. Obedience to the teachings and commandments to God leads to a wonderful Christian life characterized by peace, joy, and success. Obedience is a good practice that brings joy and harmony.

Freedom and Liberty to Pursue Happiness. We are very fortunate to live in a country like the United States of America because our Constitution provides us the freedom of the press, speech, religion, and the right to assemble. But, there is an even greater freedom that we take for granted, and that is the freedom of choice. We are made up of our own thoughts and beliefs.

Everything that we do begins as a thought, followed by decision, and then action. This is like making a plan where you start thinking what you are going to do tomorrow, writing it down, executing the plan, and making it a reality.

The thoughts that we entertain are controllable. We can change the thoughts in our minds within a fraction of a second, switching to other thoughts. This means that we can change our mood from negative to positive, from anxiety and worry to peace and calm. The chemical reactions that take place in our systems also follow our thoughts; for instance, when you see something scary. Assume you are riding in a plane that is descending because the engine lost its power. Your adrenal glands secrete more adrenaline and your heart beats fast. Your blood pressure increases and you begin to perspire. Others may start to get panicky. This is the fight or flight syndrome.

It is important to know that every cell in your body has its own intelligence, but they follow your mind, which governs your body. People who suffer from anxiety and depression dwell in their thoughts about their seemingly unsolvable problems. They think of their illness, their lack of money; and many other negative things. Consequently, they lose their self-esteem, which makes them miserable. Instead, they should be optimistic and be more positive. They should have more patience, look for solutions, ask for help from experts, and pray to God for assistance. It is the enduring patience that many times overcomes obstacles.

They do not realize that all problems are temporary resistances without which our minds will never develop to a higher level. Problems are the stimuli that cultivate and improve our minds. Without problems, our minds would deteriorate. Many do not realize that God has provided us all the essential things that we need. Problems are like puzzles; things are not in the proper order. To find their solutions, we have to search for different items and put them in their proper places. We have to be persistent in searching for solutions until the problem is solved.

We are blessed with many things in this country We are given free education from kindergarten through high school. We have libraries with thousands of books that we can learn more about the topics we choose. We have all the conveniences in our modern society including charitable organizations and the willingness to help needy citizens.

We also have many beautiful lakes and rivers where families can fish. We are also blessed with wooded areas and mountains, which are used for different purposes. All these things are free and we should thank God for all these blessings!

These are the best and the greatest things in life. They are mostly intangible and are found within us. They are the greatest assets we have. We don't have to find them or buy them, and we can use and exercise them at any time. I will end this chapter with a prayer:

Almighty God, I desire only the good and the best things in life. If it be Your will, grant me a mind that has pure thoughts, great ideals, strong faith, and the wisdom to comprehend the truth. I pray for a body that defiles evil and unrighteousness. Grant me great zeal, strength, and good health so that I can accomplish the greatest ideals of mankind.

I pray for a heart that beats with great compassion, inexhaustible patience, dedication, and a charitable heart that tenders love to all mankind.

Grant me a hand that has the warm and tender touch to heal the sick, to right the wrong, and to cheer and comfort the lonely.

Through Jesus Christ and the Holy Spirit who strengthen me, I can do all these things! So, let it be!

Chapter 22
The Greatest Credo of a Good Teenager

I will obey my parents, my teachers, and my elders, for this is the greatest expression of my love and respect for them. When I was young, I didn't have any responsibilities. Like other children, I played with my friends, sisters, and brothers. My parents were my teachers and they taught me everything. As I grew up, my o parents gave me additional responsibility and taught me how to do things right, as well as all the wholesome attitudes and good moral values. My older siblings taught me what they learned and helped me make good decisions.

I will practice honesty at all times because honesty fosters good moral values and virtues.

I will be cheerful and pleasant to everyone because it is important to be friendly and happy. Good attitudes make others feel good.

I will be enthusiastic, energetic, and active. I will be patient and persistent, as these good attitudes will help me realize my goals and ambitions. I will listen to and follow good advice. I will read good books and I will study to learn new things every day so that I can be more useful to humanity, God, and myself.

I will take care of my body through good personal hygiene, a nutritious diet, adequate exercise, and sleep. I will avoid harmful products like drugs, tobacco, and alcohol.

I will help my parents and elders complete household chores and other necessary work. This will not only keep our home beautiful, but will demonstrate that thoughtfulness and cooperation among family members is an expression of sincere love. Cooperation will bind the family in harmony and peace.

I will be involved in extracurricular activities, community civic affairs, as well as my schoolwork. I will learn about governmental affairs so that I can be a better law-abiding citizen and assume future leadership. I will learn to budget and appropriate my time wisely and properly so that my time is balanced between school, church, and other activities.

Above all, I will keep searching for truth. I will take the Lord Jesus Christ as my total source and the director of my life. I will practice His commandments and teachings because doing so is the only way to achieve a good life here on earth.

I wrote this credo of a good teenager when my children were still in grade school. During my early years at Roane General Hospital, we didn't have many doctors. There were no doctors hired by the hospital to work in the emergency room. Whenever a patient went to the emergency room, the doctor who had seen the patient before was to be called. There were several times that I was called during the night. I was also very busy during the daytime. I didn't have time to play with my children or help them do their assignments. Fortunately; all of my children excelled in academics and two of them were valedictorians.

I wanted the credo that I wrote to be ingrained in their minds and hearts as the guiding principle in their daily activities. I am so thankful that they are great children and very successful in their professions.

Chapter 23
I Believe

I believe that there is an omnipotent, omnipresent, and omniscient Power who created the Universe and possesses all that is within it. His power is infinite and immeasurable, and He is the eternal source of life, power, wisdom, beauty', treasures, and miracles.

I believe that He exists in a spiritual form. In the past, He communicated to the apostles and prophets through His voice, through Jesus Christ, through the Bible, through other people, and by spiritual methods. Spiritual communication means communicating mind-to-mind. As an example, when you ask God something mentally (by thought), He provides the answer also in your thought.

I believe that the Bible is the greatest book ever written because it contains the eternal teachings and recorded words of our God. It is the eternal living covenant that governs the whole Universe for all generations and is dedicated to the people of the world so that we may be able to live as better Christians and fulfill the will of the Lord.

I believe that human beings are created and born not only as special people in the world, but are also endowed with special qualities-more than we ever know. I believe that if we search for these qualities and learn to develop and use them for the welfare of mankind, then we can change this turbulent world to a magnificent and peaceful world. We will transform the state of our living far beyond the comprehension of our dreams and imagination.

I believe that love is the greatest weapon and the strongest instrument in the realization of our dreams and goals. It conquers and pacifies the most furious of enemies. It is the greatest force and strongest tie that binds all creatures in harmony resulting in peace and joy. It is the greatest and sweetest spoken word of all! It is the greatest healing power for depression, fear, anxiety, worry, and many psychosomatic and emotional illnesses.

I believe that true wealth and eternal riches are not found in the stock market or in one's wallet or purse, but in our own hearts and minds. It is expressed radiantly through our cheerful smiles, tender and loving words, and through our generous deeds, which are the tangible products of the applications of the intangible virtues of mankind.

I believe that true and lasting happiness cannot be bought or sold, borrowed or received. It is created within us and it is the overall sum as well as the product of all our dreams and efforts. Our true and lasting happiness can only be achieved through perfect harmony with God, the perfect universal Power from whom all blessings come.

I believe that the greatest enemies of mankind are poor attitudes, bad habits, and bad thoughts on which he/she dwells allowing the negativity to destroy mind and body.

I believe that the greatest dominant virtue responsible for the realization of our dreams and success is our faith that everything is possible with the help of God. I believe that the cause of many', if not all failures is the fear that we are not going to succeed, even if we have not yet tried.

I believe that the greatest possession of life is wisdom, which enables one to solve his/her own problems, good health to accomplish daily tasks, obligations, and responsibilities, as well as the application of the fine virtues of mankind, which enables attainment of eternal blessings.

I believe that the greatest. purpose of our earthly life is to search, develop, and apply the hidden wisdom and treasures from our infinite thoughts and minds for the benefits of mankind. We are born to improve our lives, to achieve the greatest virtues, and to experience the boundless opportunities and blessings of life while fulfilling the will of God so that we may reach the next stage of our lives, which will be eternal, blissful, affluent, and perfect! Truly, what one believes is what one may become and that is what molds one's character, integrity; and identity.

Chapter 24
The Trademark of Greatness

Greatness is not individual strength alone, nor is it intelligence or wisdom from within. It is not political heights and achievements, nor is it enormous material wealth. Greatness is the capability of having and doing all those things and the application of the fine virtues of mankind. When added together, greatness produces a beneficial effect to improve the quality of human life and works toward the glory of the Almighty God so that one may fulfill His will.

An acronym helps define GREATNESS:

G   **Generous and Godly.** It is the love for mankind, especially the meek and the poor, and the desire to work for the good of all and for the glory of our Lord Jesus Christ.

R   **Respectful and Responsible.** It is the art of courtesy and recognition and praise of one's identity and performance. It is the great capacity and concern that you have for the good of all people.

E   **Enthusiasm and Endurance.** It is the dynamic and vigorous spirit to serve and participate in the many activities designed to uplift and promote the welfare of mankind. It is the capacity to accept failure and defeat and convert them into the laurels of success.

A **Amiable and Affectionate**. That glowing and cordial charm, which draws people closer to you and makes them feel special, is important.

T **Trustworthy and Thoughtful.** This is the art and practice of communication, truthfulness, and honesty; which restores and strengthens faith and confidence.

N Nobility. The practice of dedication, prudence, humility; and forgiveness, which are attributes of good leadership.

E **Extraordinary and Expert.** This refers to the small, yet, very special effort of doing much greater work than that for which you are paid, and going above and beyond what is expected of you. It is the hallmark of benevolence and true generosity. Expertise is the ability of correcting wrongs and making the right things even better.

S **Sincerity and Sacrifice.** It is the inspired, driven purpose and the willingness to help and serve others in times of sorrows and critical needs. It is compassionate sympathy and service that enriches hopes, strengthens faith, and overcomes despair.

S **Strong and Successful.** Standing strong and firm in the commitment and fulfillment of the teachings, laws, and commandments of God and Jesus Christ. There is satisfaction of having done all these things that glorify God.

Mother Teresa, Abraham Lincoln, Albert Einstein, and former President Jimmy Carter are just a few examples of great people with these attributes. There are many others such as Oprah Winfrey; former President Bill Clinton, Mr. Bill Gates, and Mr. Warren Buffet who have donated their time and fortune to needy people in Africa. There are many others who established charitable foundations to help the needy.

Chapter 25
The "I Will" Credo of a Good Christian/Samaritan

I will not question my faith in God or His omnipresence, omnipotence, His omniscience, and His eternal existence. I will, instead, strengthen my faith by frequently and fervently praying and communicating with Him by searching His laws and teachings and will uphold and apply them as guiding principles in the affairs of my life.

I will allow only the good and fine virtues of mankind to dwell and flourish in my mind and in my heart, and I will radiate these to others by my cheerful smiles, kind words, and caring hands.

I will learn something new everyday. I will share and teach what I learned to others whenever possible.

I will remember to perform my duties and obligations to my family and my country I will set a model for others in order to establish, maintain, and strengthen our eternal love, which binds the whole family together in perfect peace and harmony bringing joy and happiness.

I will uphold what is true and let others know that the true riches and wealth in life are good health, wisdom, and the application of good virtues.

I will learn to appropriate and budget my time wisely and go that extra mile every day in order to achieve the greatest efficiency for my job and the most productive results for myself and others.

I will discipline myself to exercise moderation and temperance and to practice the rules of prudence, righteousness, faithfulness, and loving to keep my spiritual and physical body in the best condition.

I will learn the art of understanding, persistence, humility, love, and compassion, for these are the solid foundations of true success.

I will be more attentive and responsive to the needs of my society and its constituents and, whenever possible, I will help solve their problems believing that these are the attributes of a good follower and leader.

I will endeavor to accomplish and exercise all of the above plans not only for realizing monumental achievements, but because this is what I believe I was created for, to give the best and the most that I can, so help me God!

Chapter 26
A Physician's Prayer

Almighty God, Creator of life, the Greatest Healer of all:

I thank, thee, Lord, for the gift of life and the many blessings that You have given me. I thank, Thee for my profession that I may heal and relieve the sick comfort the lonely, and aide the needy. Help me, God, to use my profession wisely and to the fullest of my ability. I ask, not for miracles, but I ask for Your guidance in the thorough examinations of my patients so that I may not make errors in my diagnosis. Give me the wisdom to be able to administer the proper medicines that will result in the complete care and full recovery of my patients.

As a surgeon/physician, teach me not to make hasty decisions, yet, give me the firm courage not to resist hesitation to perform an operation or emergency intervention to save a patient's life.

Help me at all times to apply the virtues of love, kindness, and sympathy so that even in the midst of crisis and hate, I shall not fail to attend urgent calls in life-threatening situations. Teach me to put my duty above all other things so that I may help save lives. Give me the strength and inexhaustible patience so that I may be able to sustain many long hours and sleepless nights in the complicated and tedious care of my patients. Don't allow those hours to be wasted in vain, but rather make them the source of better understanding, greater enthusiasm, and more satisfaction for having done the best that I can with your help.

Guide me, dear Lord, that I shall not fail or miss anything of importance. However, if I do, let it not be a major cause of failure, but rather be the kindest allowance for Your great assistance. Grant the same, dear Lord, to the nurses, aides, and other personnel involved so that we may achieve the same goals and receive the same rewards and satisfaction.

Heavenly Father, help my patients to realize that no matter how good the medications may be, if the patient refuses to take them or is too sickly to be healed, no one can save their life. Please give them the virtue of obedience to accept the best medical care given to them. Give patients the necessary energy to heal and to combat harmful germs. Please make them whole and new.

Above all, dear Lord, grant my patients the wisdom to know the truth and righteousness so that they may live and abide by Your will and work for Your glory and, consequently, lead healthier and richer lives forevermore. I fervently ask these in the sweet name of Jesus Christ. Amen.

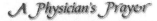

A Physician's Prayer

Almighty GOD—CREATOR of LIFE, the GREATEST HEALER of ALL and from whom all BLESSINGS COME—I thank THEE LORD for the gift of life and the MANY BLESSINGS you have given me and for my profession so that I can heal and relieve the sick, comfort the lonely and help the needy.

HELP me GOD to use my profession wisely and to the fullest of my ability. I ask not for miracles, but I ask THY GUIDANCE in the thorough examination of my patients so that I may not make any error in my diagnosis and be able to administer the proper medicines which will result in the complete cure and full recovery of my patients.

As a PHYSICIAN, TEACH me not to make a hasty decision, yet give me the firm courage not to hesitate for a moment when operation becomes mandatory in the salvation of my patient's life.

HELP me at all times to apply the virtues of LOVE, KINDNESS and SYMPATHY, so that even in the midst of CRISIS and HATE, I shall not fail to attend urgent calls and where life threatening situations are evident, teach me to put my duty first above all other things if only to do so, I can truly help and save human lives.

GIVE me the STRENGTH and inexhaustible PATIENCE so that I may be able to sustain the many long hours and sleepless nights in the complicated tedious care of my patients. Yet let not those hours be wasted in vain, but rather be the source of better understanding, greater enthusiasm and more satisfaction for having done the best that I can—realizing that the long hours spent—are the true miracle healing powers that can change the hopeless world of the patient into one with a glowing faith which leads to a new healthy life.

GUIDE me, dear LORD, that I shall not FAIL nor MISS any important medication, but if I do, let it not be a major cause of failure but rather be THY KINDEST ALLOWANCE for THY GREAT ASSISTANCE!

GRANT the same, dear LORD, to the NURSES and the AIDES and all the PERSONNEL involved so that we all can achieve the same goals and receive the same rewards and satisfaction.

Oh HEAVENLY FATHER—HELP also my patients—realizing that no matter how good the medicines may be, if the patient refuses to take them or is too weak and too sickly to be healed—none can save his life. THEREFORE give him the VIRTUE of OBEDIENCE to accept that which is the best medical care to be rendered to him, give him all the necessary energy to help all his tissues heal to help combat all the harmful germs and to melt all the unwanted cells and tumors in his systems so that he may be made NEW and WHOLE.

ABOVE all dear LORD, GRANT my patients the WISDOM to know the TRUTH and RIGHTEOUSNESS and may THEY live and abide by THY WILL, and work for THY GLORY so that they may live HEALTHIER and RICHER FOREVERMORE. I FERVENTLY ASK THESE in the SWEET name of JESUS CHRIST, Amen.

HOLY BIBLE

TEXTBOOK OF SURGERY, INTERNAL MEDICINE AND PEDIATRICS

Chapter 27
A Prayer for Self-Healing

Everything that exists in the Universe is in the form of energy and is in motion. Each object or matter be it invisible or tangible, has its own pattern of wavelength or frequencies that correspond to its energy. Those that are tangible in form, for the most part, are solid in nature and have low frequencies and wavelengths, and are subject to change and destruction, while those that are intangible have fast frequencies and are indestructible. Our cells have their own intelligence and can be controlled by our own mind or thoughts. Our thoughts and the Holy Spirit are also intangible, very powerful, and are indestructible.

So how should one pray? Matthew 6:6,7 (KJV) says: *"But thou, when thou prayest, enter into thy closet, and when thou hast shut thy door; pray to thy Father which is in secret; and thy Father which seeth in secret shall reward thee openly. But when ye pray, use not vain repetitions, as the heathen do; for they think they shall be heard for their much speaking."*

There are various books on meditation, many of which I have read in an attempt to discover the most effective way to pray so that God will favor us. I found that the best way boils down to the verses in Matthew, as quoted above. The fact that God wants us to go into our rooms and shut the door indicates that we should be in a place where we cannot be disturbed so that we may fully concentrate. When we pray we should be in a very receptive mood with utmost sincerity and faith, which makes us well through the grace of Jesus Christ. I believe that praying mentally and not orally is more effective. In other words, use only your thoughts, which are spiritual energies and in the same spiritual level as the Holy Spirit. St. John 4:24, "*God is spirit and those who worship Him must worship in spirit and in truth.*"

Here are some steps to follow when praying:

- Make peace with God. Go to a quiet room so that you can concentrate or focus better. Either sit comfortably or lie down. Relax by inhaling and exhaling slowly so that your stomach is expanding more than your chest. Doing this will allow you to relax, changing your brain waves, and approximating the wavelength of the Holy Spirit. This is the same principle as that of a radio. If you transmit or receive a message, there has to be the same common frequency.

- During your relaxation period, ask for forgiveness of all your trespasses and shortcomings. Ask the Holy Spirit to guide your thoughts and activities so that whatever you do is pleasing to God. Focus your thoughts on the many blessings that God has bestowed upon you. Thank Him for all of the beauty of the earth, the mountains, flowers, towering trees, and the vast oceans and lakes with millions of living things in them. Think of the wonderful manmade creations. Ask the Holy Spirit to be the director of your life and to help you love God with all your strength and mind and to be more humble, grateful, and appreciative for His forgiveness and steadfast love. With this preparation, you are now in better harmony with God and He will be pleased that you have that attitude. You are in a better position to obtain His healing power.

- As you inhale, tell yourself orally or in your mind that you are inhaling the most potent healing energies into your body!, directing them to the part of your body that is affected. Do this several times. Likewise, as you exhale, state that you are exhaling all the toxic and harmful chemicals in your body.

- After doing this several times, tell yourself mentally or orally that you are inhaling the love of Jesus Christ and the Holy Spirit into your body. Once you've repeated this, now tell yourself that because love is the essence of God, Jesus, and the Holy Spirit, you are united with them in spirit.

- Now request Him to heal your entire body; rid you of disease, and make you a new human being. Also, imagine that the diseased cells, if they are cancerous, are being killed or eaten by your immune cells, which are the lymphocytes, and the megakaryocytes, which are the natural killer cells. Imagine that the diseased cells are just like solid ice and are being melted by the healing energies. Claim that God created you to be a perfect human being and the Holy Spirit dwells in you, who knows no limit of what He can do for you. State in your mind and try to feel that the healing power or energy of God is now flowing throughout your body; especially in the part or parts that are diseased.
- The final step is to thank God. Tell your Creator and Savior your utmost desire to live longer, to be a new person who will always be faithful and serve God and many others who may need your love or service.

This prayer or meditation may be repeated until you are healed. Of course you have to remember that God heals in many other ways. He may use a doctor, a minister, or a dietitian, and the sick patient must cooperate with them. The strong desire to live is also a factor. I have seen and observed many people die because they don't want to live longer.

Chapter 28
The Simple Prayer of a Sick Patient

Almighty God, Creator of the Universe and the fullness thereof:

I come to You, Lord, to praise Your name and to express my sincerest and deepest gratitude for the countless blessings that You have bestowed upon me. I come to You to repent and ask for Your forgiveness for all my trespasses and shortcomings and to heal my body completely.

I have been very sick, Lord, and the use of many medicines has not helped me. You created me. You are the Source of all lives, and I will always praise You for Your infinite power, steadfast love, and mercy. I have complete and absolute faith in You, Lord, and I believe that You can heal me of my existing illness because You are the greatest physician. You can even raise the dead.

I don't exactly know how to ask You to bestow Your healing power upon me, but You know my situation and all I have to do is depend upon You. I am now asking for Your gracious mercy upon me and that You would restore my health. I pray that Your Holy Spirit would dwell in me that I might be a better person and be of better service to mankind. Thank you Lord Jesus and Almighty God! Amen.

Chapter 29
How to Read the Bible

On a beautiful, quiet Easter Sunday in 1973, I flew to Harvard Medical School to attend a three-week course review in general surgery As I waited for my plane to Boston, questions flooded my mind. Earlier that day, I had decided to quit smoking. I realized how poisonous it was and promised myself I'd never again light one up. I had not experienced how bad smoking was until I climbed up to the fifth floor because the elevator of the hospital was not working. I felt a little short of breath while the rest of my colleagues were unaffected. I had smoked a long time, perhaps twenty years, averaging one pack a day. I thought that this would be a good time to quit; after all, no one was allowed to smoke inside a lecture room.

I worried about withdrawal. Would it be as bad as everyone said? Would I feel or think crazy? Would I be irritable-or worse? I would rather go back to smoking than harm anyone. I was more concerned, though, with having to go back to school. I had finished my surgical residency five years before. On the other hand, there is progress in medical science every year and what better way to stay abreast than to go to Harvard Medical School, which is one of the best institutions. I always wanted to know or learn what was new because I desired to always render the best treatment for my patients. Mysteriously; it seemed as if someone was addressing me, which I had never experienced before.

"My son, what do you know about true life? You only know a little bit about parts of your body; a little bit about how they work:, and a little bit about disease and treatment. You don't really know the better and greater part of life, which is the spiritual life."

I answered back mentally; realizing that I didn't know much. Maybe I had not read enough of my Bible to truly understand it. I asked how I could learn more about the spiritual life.

"I am glad you asked that question, Son, and I am glad that you are going to Boston to study more about medicine and surgery I also praise you for having brought three books with you to read, which I am sure may also change your thinking on success. In the next few days, you will learn with me, and I will answer every question that you ask me."

Shortly after lunch I arrived at my hotel, a block away from Massachusetts General Hospital, where the lectures were to be conducted. As I was settling into the room, I noticed a Gideon Bible on top of the dresser. I grabbed it, sat down, and quickly began flipping through it at random. To my surprise, I focused my eyes on the very verses that were the answers to every question I asked. I studied the Bible every day and continued to find answers for all the questions that I had. I was so thrilled and I felt like a new person endowed with a special wisdom that I never had before. I never had the least doubt that God was talking to me through the Bible.

One evening, I passed by a bookstore and saw a book entitled Cosmic Consciousness. I bought the book and added it to the list that I read. There was also a publication containing ten pages about Kirlian photography; which was developed by a Russian scientist, Dr. Kirlian. This type of photography is taking a picture of the human aura, the energy that emanates from our body. Since then, I have read and learned more about the human aura, the energy emanating from almost every living creatures including living plants. All the books that I read were so interesting that I found myself reading the entire night without the need for sleep. Overall, I must have read four or five books during that three-week span.

With regards to my smoking, not only did I not smoke again, but I did not experience any withdrawal symptoms. Since that experience, I have read the Bible many times, but understanding verses takes a lot of concentration and I am going to share with you my method for reading the Bible. First, though, I'd like to express my beliefs about the Bible.

I truly and honestly believe that the Bible is the living guidebook of life for all generations. It is the greatest book ever published because the real author is God, through His Holy Spirit, who guided the apostles and other writers. It is a great book because it has transformed many lives from wastefulness, sorrow, and misery to hope, peace and joy. It transforms us from ignorance to enlightenment and from failure to success. Because God is our Creator, He loves us and has a plan for us.

The Bible was written and meant to exist from creation to eternity so that He may manifest His infinite love for us and all mankind for the past, present, and future generations. He wants all mankind to understand that if we love God and follow his teachings and commandments, we will have a better and wonderful life, glorified with peace, good health, and happiness.

Most households have at least one Bible, but many people probably don't read it as often as they should. I am not sure if we understand everything we read. I, personally have difficulty understanding some of the verses I read, but we can pray for God's guidance while reading. If we accept the Bible as God's written voice or words and abide by its guiding principles, then there is no doubt the Bible will transform our lives for the better, allowing us to experience the Holy Spirit and His infinite love.

So, how do we read the Bible to experience its power? First, make an appointment with God as you would if you were making an appointment for a job interview or physician's visit. A time and place should be specified. The place should be free of interruptions and distractions. Consider this appointment as the greatest and most important teaching period of your life because you are meeting with the Holy Spirit of God as your teacher. You should be punctual and in a receptive mood. Your desire to learn, absorb, and understand every word of God should be comparable to the desire of a man who has gone days without water and all he desires is to drink.

Before you open your Bible, hold it close to your chest and pray. Pray for a desire to be a son or daughter of God, that you want a peaceful, joyful, healthy, and successful life. Pray for an understanding of God's words so that you may be able to abide by His will. You may study the Bible by subjects or by books. Make sure you are focused on the study subject for the time period. After your session with God, express gratitude to Him and pray that you'll be able to apply everything that you learned.

Follow the same method each time you want to study the Bible. The most important thing is applying what you read and learn. God will be watching you to see whether you follow His teachings. If you violate them, He will be very disappointed and you may not experience His love, power, or presence. On the other hand, if you remain faithful and follow His teachings, He will be excited and will manifest Himself to you and He will bless you and empower you. This has been my method of studying the Bible; use it and perhaps God will bless you for it!

Chapter 30
Spend a Little Time

Spend a little time . . . praying. It is the best way to communicate with your Creator, God. It is the reflection of your Christian identity.

Spend a little time . . . getting to know yourself. Renew and evaluate your daily performances. Include your moods, habits, and attitudes. Grade or compare yourself to any acceptable standard pattern. By knowing your weaknesses, unhealthy or unpleasant habits, you can rid yourself of them and replace them with the fine virtues of mankind.

Spend a little time . . . reading, studying, and learning. This is one of the best ways to further your knowledge and gain more wisdom, provided you practice and live the new knowledge you have learned.

Spend a little time . . . exercising. You can walk, run, cycle, dance, swim, lift, or participate in other rigorous activities. This is the secret to good health.

Spend a little time . . . smiling and saying hello. This is the greatest gesture of friendship, which leads you on the road to happiness.

Spend a little time . . . giving tithe or donation to charity. Giving back indicates that we are blessed. Charity brings faith, hope, courage, and prosperity.

Spend a little time . . . communicating with friends and relatives. Thoughtfulness strengthens the bonds of relationship, friendship, and brings families closer together.

Spend a little time . . . in community service. Such as serving in the hospital auxiliary, helping in the library, or assisting with your local emergency squad. This gives you the opportunity to serve your fellow citizens and get to know more people.

Spend a little time . . . attending church. Church attendance enhances your opportunity to know and gain more friends and helps you learn more about God and His will. They may be your great support group in case of need.

Spend a little time . . . engaged in a hobby. Write, play; collect, or explore. This makes life more satisfying.

Spend a little time . . . treasuring your senses. Smell the sweet fragrance of a rose, hear the birds sing early in the morning, and watch as the breeze blows through the trees.

Most importantly, spend a little time . . . expressing gratitude to God. Thank Him for the many blessings He has bestowed upon you. Thank Him for your friends and family who bring you joy.

Chapter 31
Today

Today is the most important day of your life.

Today's steps are all you need to take.

Today's challenges are all you need to meet.

Today's decisions are all you need to make.

Tomorrow is the next episode in a great adventure; it comes heralding its own good, but the present is here now.

Today, live to the fullest.

Today, exert your best effort.

Today, laugh in the sunshine of God's love.

Today, savor the sights, sounds, and smells of life.

Today, diligently apply the lessons you have learned in the past.

Today, take advantage of the opportunity to serve, love, understand, and grow in cosmic consciousness.

When today is finished, lay it gratefully aside and thank

God for today's unique experience. There will never be another day like today!.

Today, one should be the very best at whatever he/she wishes to do.

Today, complete all of the things that you have planned such as writing your last will and testament or other things that build your legacy.

Today is the only opportunity one can truly have because yesterday is gone and tomorrow is only a vision.

Life is so fragile and critical and we don't know when the last moment of our life will take place.

Hence one should take time today to pray for forgiveness and for God to take care of your loved ones.

Chapter 32
The Greatest Virtue: Love

To be sincere, honest, and truthful.
To be patient, persistent, and persevering.
To be loyal, faithful, and abiding.
To be prudent, righteous, and upright.
To be understanding, considerate, and forgiving.
To be kind, sympathetic, and enduring.
To be friendly; cheerful, and cordial.
To be creative, flexible, and resourceful.
To be industrious, diligent, and dedicated.
To be active, enthusiastic, and dynamic.

These virtues are the finest threads of love and wisdom, which, when woven together and applied, become a beautiful fabric, the eternal and the crowning emblem of a good Christian.

I like to quote here the "Gift of Love" from the Book of 1 Corinthians 13: 1-13.

If I speak in the tongues of mortals and of angels, but do not have love, I am a noisy gong or a clinging cymbal. And if I have prophetic powers and understand all mysteries and all knowledge, and if I have all faith, so as to remove mountains, but do not have love, I am nothing. If I gave away all my possessions, and if I hand over my body, so that I may boast. But do not have love, I gain nothing. Love is patient, love is kind, love is not envious, or boastful or arrogant or rude.

It does not insist on its way; it is not irritable or resentful; it does not rejoice in wrongdoing but rejoices in truth. It bears all things, endures all things. Love never ends. But as for prophecies, they will come to an end,' as for tongues; they will cease; as for knowledge, it will come to an end. For we know only in part; and we prophesy only in part; but when the complete comes, the partial will come to an end. When I was a child, I spoke like a child, I thought like a child; I reasoned like a child; when I became an adult, I put an end to childish ways. For now we see in a mirror dimly, but then we see face to face. Now I know only in part; then I will know fully, even as I have been fully known. And now faith, hope and love abide, these three, and the greatest of these is LOVE.

Chapter 33
Almighty Father, I Believe in You

Almighty Father, I believe in You.
Though I don't see Your Face and I don't hear Your Voice,
I see You in my mind.
I hear You and feel You in my heart!

Yes, Lord God, I believe in You.
I feel Your infinite love every moment of my life.
I read Your treasury of unspoken words in the Bible.
I read the many books and poems that your disciples wrote.
I feel the strength of your hands when You guide me in major
    surgeries.

Almighty God, I believe in You.
I see Your unique personality in the manifestation of the sweetest
    word called "LOVE".
I see the greatness of Your Power in the wonders and beauty of the
    human life.
I see Your infinite power in the beauty of the Universe and the
    countless forms of life that exist in the planets.
I read that You presented yourself in the gentle face of Jesus Christ.

Yes, Almighty Father, I believe in You.
When I am alone, You provide me Your Spirit as my company.

When I am in trouble, You help me.
When I am sick, You healed me.
When I am at my best, You use me!

Almighty God, I believe in You.
And because I do,
I love You more than I can say and do.
I know You are everywhere, watching me.
I know that You provide the answer to every problem,
The fulfillment of every need and the things I have asked.

Yes, Almighty Father, I believe in You.
I praise Your sweet name everyday.
I give Thee my thanks for helping and guiding me.
I am very grateful for my life for sending me out here in this little
    world.
Above all, I am grateful and happy because of what You are!

I wrote the above poem because I felt God had abandoned me. I lost so much money in a company that I founded, "The American Oil & Gas Company." This was in 1980-82 when the oil prices went up so high. A friend whom I have known for several years and also a patient of mine was to be in charge, as I didn't have the time to supervise. He told me that he knew everything about the oil business as he had worked in oil drilling all his life. He told me that there was a lot of oil in West Virginia and it was just a matter of digging it out. He stated that he could rent the machine so cheap as well as personnel to help him out. I believed and trusted all that he told me and so I borrowed all the capital from a bank with eighteen percent interest, which was the ongoing interest at that time. I trusted him, but it turned out that he was not good at managing. I truly felt that he scammed me. I have not recovered a single cent of what I borrowed.

I felt so depressed and I asked myself, Where is my God who had always been good to me? I filed a suit against him, but the lawyer whom I hired was a good friend of his father and, despite the expensive cost of the fee I paid him, I failed to recover my money. There was nothing else that I could do but to forget that big mistake.

Out of my distress, I expressed my faith to God in the poem that I wrote above. That in my heart He will always be my only Great God and that without His love and guidance in my life, I am nothing. I am currently taking a discipleship class that makes my faith and relationship with Him even stronger and closer. I know that He is always in control of major catastrophic events including the rise and fall of kingdoms or nations in this world.

Chapter 34
The Meaning of Christmas

Christmas is one of the best seasons of the year. It is the season of great anticipation and excitement of every child who is looking forward, hoping and praying that Santa Claus will come with a bag full of candy and toys. It is a moment of great remembering and reflection on all of our friends and loved ones. It is the loveliest day of the year, not only because of the flurries of snow coming from heaven or because every home is gorgeously decorated with multi-colored, glittering lights and the atmosphere is reverberating with the tunes of Christmas songs, but because it is also the most peaceful moments in everyone's life that even the guns on the warfront become quiet and silent in order for them to express their grateful thanks and prayers for the birth of JESUS CHRIST especially for HIS ministry, teaching, healing, and for having saved the sinners.

Christmas has so many meanings indeed, but I found it best to interpret it by giving the meaning of each alphabetical letter:

C   stands for **CHRIST**: the LORD JESUS, who was born in a manger in the town of Bethlehem-whose birth, wisdom, and teaching have become the greatest influence amongst mankind in the past to the present and into the future.

H   is for the great **HOLIDAY** to honor and celebrate the great MESSIAH who became the greatest man in the history of mankind.

R is for **REFRESHING** and **REJOICING** among all Christians as well as for remembering and strengthening the bonds of love and friendship among relatives, loved ones, and friends.

I is for **INSPIRING** moments in the life of the great prophets, disciples, and Christian leaders who paved the way for the coming of the Messiah, the LORD CHRIST:

S is for **SALVATION** of the sinners and the forgiveness of their sins so that they may have a chance to dwell in GOD'S heavenly kingdom.

T is for **TIME** to celebrate and be thankful and grateful for the countless blessings we all enjoy, which are the greatest gifts from the Almighty FATHER.

M is the **MOMENT** of peace throughout the world and sending and receiving gifts and cards to and from our friends and families, thereby refreshing relationships.

A is for the **ALMIGHTY GOD**, the FATHER, who gave HIS only begotten son, JESUS CHRIST that whosoever believes in HIM shall not perish, but have an everlasting life.

S is for **SPIRITUAL** development and the uplifting of all men. It is the time for uniting our thoughts in perfect harmony with the DIVINE POWER, so that joy and happiness will be complete and be felt in our lives.

Chapter 35

My Best Insurance and Inheritance
from My Parents

To: My Father, Andres Bautista Gamponia and
   My Mother, Julia Lafrades Gamponia

My Darling Parents:
   Death is an inevitable transition from the physical substance to the
spiritual form. I know that you will exist eternally in the same way that
you are most treasured forever in my thoughts, in my soul, and deep
in my heart.
   You left me no will, but you gave me all the love you had when I
was young and growing. Yes, mother dear, I will always remember the
day you went to pick vegetables for four hours on our farm and carried
it on your head for almost two miles to the market. You sold the entire
basket of fruit and of vegetables, and when I asked for a quarter you
gave it all to me without even asking what I needed it for.
   But more than that, you never ceased to kneel and pray every
morning before you began your day and again in the evening before
you laid down fingering your rosary beads one after the other. One
time I asked what you were praying for and you said, "I always pray for
the blessing of the Lord that our family remains healthy and that you
will succeed in whatever vocation you choose."

I also remember you reading to me the Bible. Every year, even though I was not home, you always celebrated my birthday. You always cooked nice cakes, invited all our neighbors, lit a candle, and prayed for my success and good health. I never asked you how far you went to school, but I knew in my heart that you were blessed with a virtue that was unmatched.

The word **conscientious**, **dedicated** and **responsible** were boldly written in your heart and never faltered or faded under any circumstance! Truly you were an angel sent from above!

And, Dad, I never saw one as strict a disciplinarian as you. Even just a little mistake I made, I agonized with the scolding words you made. Each time you worked you always called me to watch and help you that I might learn whatever you made. I finally realized that you did so because you loved me so much. You taught me many basic skills that I would never learn elsewhere, not even in a Boy Scout class. I am really grateful that you taught me all those things so that I don't have to depend on someone else. You both left me no trace of gold or fragments of silver or diamonds, but you taught me to love and enjoy the arts and dignity of labor and responsibility so that I may survive in all adversities.

You both gave me no dowry but you have labored and sacrificed hard to send me to schools so that I could not only gain wisdom but to use it well for the benefit of mankind. Yes, I remember how difficult and meager our life was. You raised me and sent me to college with untold sacrifices not knowing where to get or borrow money for my next tuition. But the Lord had always been very good. He always enabled us to find a way to borrow money somewhere. When I graduated as a doctor, what an exciting time it was! The entire town celebrated gratefully!. And at long last, a one-time poor kid growing up gathering and carrying a big basketful of grass for two horses every afternoon after a high school class, now saw a long line of sick patients every day.

Above all, you both taught me the greatest virtues: the ability to love and serve mankind the best I can and the persistent desire to learn and fulfill the will of God so that I may forever dwell in righteousness, which is the only path to that most coveted glorious life!

There are no greater values beyond those great inheritances and, indeed, they are worthy of the greatest emulation through all eternity. I am most grateful to both of you and may God keep us lovingly together in His spiritual kingdom!

Chapter 36
Friendship

It is a relationship of one to another. It can be one of the most treasured possessions, provided it is not abused. True and faithful friends are sometimes more than a brother or a sister. Usually, they have common attitudes, habits, and activities and these things tighten and strengthen their relationship. For instance, a group of women who are good friends get together a few days or evenings, play cards, or join together to make a certain project such as making a quilt. There are also groups of boys who gather together and play basketball in their yard or play games with their computers. They really enjoy each other's company. Together, they talk about each other's successes and failures and share the good things they have learned.

I have always enjoyed the company of my smart classmates in college because I learned from them. Sometimes, we got together before our final examination to ask many questions and answered them correctly in preparation for the exam.

When one receives an honor, his/her friends share the honor and they rejoice and celebrate. I got involved in politics at our school and, for no reason, I always won by a landslide. In the evening following the election, all my friends dragged me to the best restaurant, had drinks, and ordered the best items available on the menu.

I have seen friends who would exchange or give each other a dress, necktie, or shirt that they had because their friend liked it so much. When one of their friends got sick or lost their spouse, they would visit frequently to comfort, to help, and provide what is needed. I know someone whose house burned, and in no time, the friends offered for them to stay with them in their house, gave them clothes and other things they needed. They brought joy to each other.

Friends are excited when they see each other. They maintain close and frequent contact by way of communication regardless of the thousand miles distance. They long to see each other after a few times of missed association. If one is sick or needs help, the other sets a special time to render service or other needs and enjoys doing so. They go to see their favorite movie, go shopping, and eat at their favorite restaurant. They go to the same church and even ride together to save gas. If their houses are close to each other and one goes on a long trip, the good friend volunteers to watch and take care of the other's house and pets.

When is friendship abused? It is abused when one keeps taking advantage of the other.

There are doctors who are partners and are supposed to work during their scheduled dates but, instead, they would leave and go somewhere even though the schedule was very busy. There were a couple of surgeons who worked in the same hospital. One of the surgeons always kept asking the other surgeon to cover for him because of such and such. Both surgeons were supposed to be paid whenever they work. The one surgeon would leave town when he was supposed to work. The problem was that the surgeon who left town kept the money instead of volunteering to give it to the surgeon who worked for him. I believe that the surgeon not only abused the nice guy, but also manipulated him. This is inexcusable. The abused surgeon should have reported it to the administration and claim that he should receive the money whenever he works the other surgeon's shift unless they have a mutual agreement that is fair for both of them.

Chapter 37
What Makes a Mason

What makes a Mason is not race nor breed; it is not strength or power, neither financial wealth nor royal dynasty. We all possess the same flesh and bone as well as the same breath of life, which is a gift from the Divine Master. Perhaps the true meaning of MASONRY is best described briefly by what each alphabetical letter stands for:

M   **Man.** A man who is raised, educated, and passed through rigorous training in the graded portals of Divine wisdom patterned after the Church of St. John in Jerusalem.

A   **Active.** He is active in the pursuit of educating, enlightening, and helping his brethren. He is also active in service especially to the destitute and needy for the uplifting of his fellowmen.

S   **Sincere.** He is sincere and honest in all his ways. Strong, not only in his own grip, but also his conviction; sacrificing, always willing to contribute his time and effort for the relief of his distressed brethren. o Oneness. Oneness with God whom he faithfully accepts as his Creator and Savior. Having squared his passions and actions, and having strengthened and leveled his thoughts into perfect harmony with the teachings of Jesus Christ, he now developed his strong faith in God, which leads him to a peaceful life!

N Nobility. He has noble thoughts and a noble heart because he has compassion; he practices humility, temperance, prudence, and fortitudes, which are the crowning virtues of a great Christian leader!

For those who do not know or understand what Masonry is, it is a brotherhood much like a fraternity and it is a worldwide organization. Its main function is to establish better relations among the members and to help one another in times of need. Each member receives a special symbol like the way each one shakes hands or knocks on a door. A member also wears a specific ring according to his level of education. For example, one who finishes a third degree wears a ring with a pyramid shape, dark emblem and the inside is the shape of a flame.

When the member finishes the thirty-second degree, he wears a double eagle sign on his ring. There is also a special ring for a o thirty-third degree. This degree is conferred to one who is dedicated and who received further training. After one has a thirty second degree, he is eligible to become a Beni Kedem Shriner and he has to undertake and pass additional lessons.

The highest rank among the Shriners is the Potentate who is elected by the members. Candidates for Mason have to be recommended by an active member of the lodge who presents an application. The whole membership of the lodge will discuss the application and acceptance is based on a unanimous vote.

The Beni Kedem is a charitable organization and supports all the best hospitals for burn cases. There is also a hospital in Kentucky, which takes care of musculoskeletal problem such as correction of physical deformities like poliomyelitis and other orthopedic problems. The hospitalization and care are free.

Chapter 38
The Greatest Discovery of All
An Unusual Experience

Citizens of the Earth:

Behold this truth and knoweth that here at last is a discovery for which you may have been searching for a thousand ages. This revelation is the climax of all human wisdom and endeavors. It is the greatest ambition ever dreamed of and the greatest aspiration of all mankind. It is a discovery that will lead you to the place everyone talks about, the place none can equal in beauty and where all the real riches and true wealth abound infinitely and where life exists in eternal splendor of peace, perfect health and lasting happiness.

As I reveal to you this discovery, listen carefully and inscribe into the tabernacle of your heart and deep into your soul. Observe and practice it every moment of your life with utmost honesty and sincerity. To despise and ignore this revelation is to lose your only opportunity and all the failures and miseries may come to you.

Here is the discovery-the path to heaven, the glorious kingdom of the good Lord. I will tell you "what, where, and how" to build and get to that path.

What? It is a very special road. Its foundation is made of the strongest steel of love and faith and the gravels and cements are chosen from the finest virtues of mankind. The water that mixes them floweth from the eternal spring of the Tell Commandments. The strength of the road is indestructible by any known or unknown force. It is the hardest road to build, yet it is the cheapest and it doesn't cost a penny!. It is difficult to find, yet it is within your reach. It is most sacred and it is invisible. It can only be perceived by your higher sense.

Where? It is built within the diamonds of the mind and extends across the breadth of thy soul. It is held and supported by the million forces and energies liberated by every beat of thy heart. It is reinforced every day by the abundant grace of the Lord and it is cleansed every day by your fervent prayer and meditation. The road can be long or short, broad or narrow, smooth or rugged; it all depends on how you build it.

How? Before I strive along this road to reach out a glimpse of that kingdom, I attune my body, my mind and my soul into one perfect harmony with the Almighty Universal Mind. I think of nothing but the infinite wonders and beauties of the Universe, the perfect and infinite miracles of life and the unique and unequal mighty powers of the Lord creator. I think of nothing but His infinite wisdom and His enormous love for me. And I keep thinking and praying how I can serve Him best. And before I realize it, I find myself at the very heart of His kingdom!

Now that you know, I ask you to build and travel that road every moment of your life. No one can build it, but you alone! It will be the greatest achievement you have accomplished in your life and the very best above all things life can possess. Yes, knoweth in your heart that it is the only road that will lead you to the most beautiful world of all the worlds!

The above essay was written on a Sunday after my lunch. We were discussing about heaven in our church Bible class, how one can get there and what heavenly life looks like. My mind kept thinking about it. My mind was so inspired that I grabbed a notebook and scribbled a few words not even thinking what words I would write. It was as if someone was holding my pen and kept writing. After it was finished, I thought it was a fairly good essay and, so, I kept it in my writing collection.

Chapter 39
Experience: A Great Teaching Lesson

The popular saying, "Experience is the best teacher," is not only a wise statement but in my experience, it is true. There are so many teenagers today who want to experience the unknown, although they may have been warned that such an act is not only destructive, but also unlawful and punishable.

Such things as taking cocaine, marijuana, or making methamphetamine are not only destructive to health, but also a crime. Such a bad experience may cause them not only addiction, but also death. Once when I was in practice, I had a case of anterior scalene muscle syndrome. This is a case characterized by tingling or even pain at a certain position of the upper extremity due to compression of the nerve by the anterior scalene muscle. The procedure is so simple but, because I had not done it before, I had to review the anatomy of the structures in the neck and the relation of the anterior scalene muscle and the nerve it compresses. If I had done it before, I would not have wasted my time studying that particular anatomy.

Likewise, people who are successful don't just buy stock because the ads on that stock are so powerful and convincing. There are so many scams these days that if you don't investigate the advertised ads, you end up losing. There are even stocks that don't really exist. I received at least three letters this month enticing me to pay a processing fee, so that I can get a grant of as much as $50-$250 thousand. They claim that their "Gate Way Foundation" gives thousands of dollars every year.

Other letters that I have received claimed that I just won a big prize worth $1.5 million, but I need to pay $50 first as a processing fee before they will send it to me. Everything that one does without having done it before creates a liability to make mistakes. For instance, when I was learning to type on a computer, I happened to touch something on the keyboard by accident, not even knowing which letter I had touched. And what happened? I lost all the sentences, which I was about to finish. What a frustration it was! I had to rewrite that letter which took me another 30 minutes.

Even just assembling furniture without reading the instructions and just looking at the pictures, it looks so easy. But, putting the parts together and in the right order makes a person not have to redo it over and over. Building a house or anything that one does for the first time makes it so difficult that the outcome may not turn out to be properly done.

I know of some newly graduated CNPs (Certified Nurse Practitioners) and even doctors who just started practicing their profession on their own without a supervisor or attendant telling them what to do. They cannot recall the medicine that is supposed to be given to the patient. I have had several calls in the past asking me what was good for such and such. Even doctors have to have experience before they graduate. They spend a year of internship by going to the hospital as early as their second year to experience taking patient history and examining patients. A hospital or other high position may not accept you unless you have experience.

I have also observed many politicians delivering their first few campaign speeches. They sometimes stumbled or didn't use the best words to express what was meant. However, they continued to get better and better as they delivered more speeches.

I recall one occasion when I had the honor of assisting in repairing a hernia in the groin. While watching, the attendant told me that it was about time for me to do the surgery I couldn't believe it myself that my fingers, holding the knife, refused to cut the skin. My attendant kept telling me to please start. I finally made the incision with fear, but again, I didn't know what to do next. I knew the different steps that I needed to take, but I could not explain why I felt that way. Of course, the more I did, the more I became an expert and even did it under local anesthesia.

I was able to send the patient home an hour after his surgery.

I do believe that everyone who does things for the first time is bound to make an error or subject themselves to fear and reluctance. It requires prudence and lots of practice like learning to play an instrument or doing carpentry. Even an athlete requires a lot of practice before one becomes the best that he or she can be.

There are also many scams today that send you a letter stating they have a "charitable foundation," which gives large sums of money for any purpose, but you must pay a processing fee of $50 before they can send you an application. After the fee was sent, you don't hear from them anymore and your letter of inquiry comes back stamped, NO SUCH ADDRESS. Likewise, many investors are being scammed. One may receive a very persuasive advertisement that a company continues to have an increase in their sales and the profit will skyrocket in the next few months only to declare bankruptcy later.

This is the typical case of the Enron Company who published a report in a newspaper only to declare bankruptcy a few months later. What happened? All of the investors, including their employees, lost all of their invested money as well as the pension of their long-time employees. This happened not only to Enron, but other companies as well.

Truly, experience is knowledge with power in action.

Chapter 40
The Blueprint for a Successful Businessman

Today; I shall live a new life. I shall forget that I only exist as an ordinary individual. Like an architect, I shall make a blueprint for my life, designed to achieve success.

I shall explore and develop the infinite talents and powers within me, which God has eternally bestowed upon me since my birth. Each day I shall devote a special time to the creation and development of new ideas. I shall screen and execute only the ideas that can best serve humanity and glorify God. I will pursue business goals that work toward providing the most needs of the people in my community. Once I have chosen that specific vocation, I will explicitly write down all the plans and how to achieve the business goals in the shortest amount of time and by the most effective means. In order to do this, I will thoroughly study every detail of the plan. In order to minimize error as well as cost, I will seek counsel from those Wil0 have achieved similar goals or have proven to be successful in this field. In addition, I will learn about business management to provide me additional insight including business law and requirements provided by the chamber of commerce such as licensing, taxes, etc.

Depending upon the initial funding, I will start a small business variety store and will continue to expand the inventories most needed.

Once the operation has begun, I will employ competent personnel who share my vision and who will operate the business on the basis of his/her unquestionable good moral conduct, good health, and capabilities, as well as dedication and devotion to their work. All employees will have adequate training for their specific job.

I will make sure that the quality of service is never tarnished with greed or selfishness for this is the root of criticism, failure, and misery. Rather, the management and operations will always be guided by love, faith, divine understanding, and patience, which are the indestructible foundations of wealth and success.

The company or its activities will be established in different states and will be constantly expanded and diversified in the hope of realizing better and greater services for the welfare of mankind in addition to providing good jobs for many honest and dedicated individuals.

Its greatest assets will be those that satisfy and fulfill the will of God so that life can be eternally richer, more peaceful, and glorious!

Such companies as Wal-Mart, Kmart, Home Depot, Lowe's, pharmacies, medical clinics, banks, and ATMs as well as modest restaurants, would all be located in the same building or on the same compound.

Chapter 41
Lifestyle Changes

Lifestyle changes are very common words among health professionals these days. This is because they are learning more about the many risk factors, which are responsible for the increasing incidence of diabetes, coronary heart disease, stroke, cancers, osteoarthritis, and many neurodegenerative disorders such as Alzheimer's disease, Parkinson's disease, Amyotrophic Lateral Sclerosis, to name a few. Despite the many advances of medicine, still the incidence of different cancers, obesity and diabetes keeps rising. The incidence of overweight among adults has increased to 65 percent, for morbid obesity to 31 percent, and overweight children to 23 percent.

While lifestyle changes have been the popular advice by health providers, patients do not follow or they lack the knowledge on how they should change their habits as well as their attitudes. Hence, they persist in doing what they have been accustomed to not realizing the long-term consequences. These patients certainly need a thorough education. They need to know how to go about transforming their lives, how they acquire various illnesses. They need to know that once the patient acquires the disease, it may not be reversible any more. The treatment will be very expensive, and may not help to prolong or improve the quality of their life.

So, how can one go about changing one's lifestyle? The first thing one must do is to know all about one's self. Look in the mirror and analyze one's self thoroughly. Focus on the bad thoughts, bad habits, bad attitudes and other bad activities and make an inventory on those. Or make an inventory of those bad thoughts, bad habits, bad attitudes and other bad activities.

Likewise, they should make an inventory of their good attitudes, or characteristics, and good habits. Bad attitudes include: selfishness, vanity, arrogance, disrespect, hypocrisy, hate, obstinacy, lack of discipline, ignorance about healthy lifestyle, dishonesty, impatience, judging, gossiping, disobedience, and stubbornness. Examples of bad habits are smoking, excessive alcohol use, lack of exercise, sedentary lifestyle (too much television or video games, procrastination, and unwillingness to read books to educate themselves about becoming healthy or becoming a better Christian.

Examples of the good attitudes and good habits are the opposites of the above poor attitudes and habits. All of those bad habits and attitudes should be replaced with good or wholesome behaviors such as love, kindness, gentleness, cooperation, industriousness, self-discipline, humility, honesty, sincerity, and passion to have a better life. One should be aware of the enormous benefits of having a healthy diet.

Smoking and drinking alcohol in excess may be the most difficult bad habits to quit because they are addictive. Therefore, one should not hesitate to see a doctor who is best able to help them. Not knowing the negative consequences of the bad habits does not allow one to make an informed decision to quit smoking or drinking. Emphasis should be placed on the fact that smoking is a high risk factor for many diseases such as cancers of the lung and throat, heart attack, stroke, high blood pressure, Alzheimer's disease, cancer of the colon, breast, prostate, and emphysema.

Smoking is also very expensive. The odor of the smoke clings to one's clothing and may become almost intolerable to someone close by. All these diseases maybe avoided if the individual doesn't smoke and, instead, adopts a healthy lifestyle. Others may stay away from the smoker to avoid secondhand inhalation of the smoke, as there are situations of those who develop lung cancer due to exposure to the smoke.

Likewise, wasting a lot of time as a couch potato (sitting on the couch watching TV all or most of the time, one may develop obesity, muscle wasting (atrophy), and osteoporosis. There are many medical problems related to obesity such as heart attack, diabetes, hypertension, sleep apnea, gallbladder disease, cancers, osteoarthritis, and osteoporosis.

Because a person is very heavy, they can hardly walk and cannot do adequate exercises.

The complications of osteoporosis include multiple fractures of the vertebra and hips, and if there are compressions of the nerves, one may have constant back pain. A fracture of the hip or even degenerative arthritis may lead to difficulty walking, constant pain, and if a hip replacement is necessary; another surgery might be required in the future, not to mention the possible complications of the surgery.

The benefits of exercise are many. It maintains and strengthens the tone of all the muscles. It increases mineral density of the bones, thereby preventing one from having osteoporosis and less of a tendency to bone fractures. It prevents hardening of the arteries, which is responsible for heart attack, high blood pressure, stroke, kidney failure, and may affect other organs. It also improves the immune systems, which enables one to be more resistant to infection. It improves one's mental health because it is known to regenerate the brain cells. It also improves the functions of the endocrine glands, especially the sex organs. It helps burn the excess fat in the body so you will not become overweight. It makes the tissues sensitive to insulin, thereby preventing diabetes or insulin resistant diabetes, the so-called metabolic syndrome.

On excess alcohol drinking, it will not only lead to addiction, but also cirrhosis of the liver, cancer of the liver, and mental deterioration. Cirrhosis of the liver leads to esophageal varices, which, if ruptured, may lead to massive bleeding and instant death. Also, cirrhosis causes chronic anemia with body weakness, ascites, hypoproteinemia, and malnutrition.

How about your dietary habits? Do you eat plenty of fried potatoes, red meat, or steak cooked over a grill? How often do you eat fruits and vegetables? Do you eat in restaurants where you go back as many times you wish for the same price? Do you eat a lot of cake, ice cream, candies, or do you add sugar or aspartame (artificial sweeteners) to your coffee? If the answers to the above questions are strongly positive, then those are the reasons why you are overweight or cannot lose weight. Carbohydrates, especially the simple and refined carbohydrates like sugar, have a high glycemic index, which is responsible for obesity. Sugar is easily absorbed into the bloodstream, which initiates the pancreas to secrete plenty of insulin in order to balance the level of sugar in the blood. More insulin in the blood, however, stimulates the craving to eat. The more you eat, the more carbohydrates are in the blood, so much that the excess is converted into fat, which makes up the adipose tissue.

The meat that is cooked over a grill has been known to produce nitrosamines, which are carcinogenic, i.e., substances that may cause cancer. One of the best ways to live long and stay healthy is to have an ideal weight. This can be achieved by eating a low-calorie diet. That is to say eat more fruits, which are complex carbohydrates. Eat more vegetables. Eating more fruits and vegetables is healthy because they provide the vitamins, minerals, and enzymes, as well as fibers that our body needs. Also, be aware how you cook your food. Overcooked foods will loose their nutrients. Steamed vegetables are the best. Also, if the foods are edible when raw, eat them as raw, but make sure they are well cleaned. Eating the raw foods preserve their chlorophyll, enzymes, and other phytonutrients, which are crucial for the nutrition of our cells.

Do you really want to stay healthy? Be aware that as you grow older, especially when you reach fifty years of age and above, you are prone to develop various illnesses related to aging. Age is a risk factor for lung, prostate, and colon cancer, Alzheimer's, osteoporosis, eye problems, heart attack, arteriosclerosis, and many other effects of mitochondrial dysfunction (failure to produce energy substances, ATP). Most of the noted conditions are preventable and also curable, if detected earl~ Many of the noted conditions have specific risk factors. I have already discussed the effects of smoking, sedentary lifestyle, and nutrition.

Prevention of colorectal and prostate cancers requires yearly rectal examinations, screening for occult blood in the stools, and a colonoscopy to check for polyps or any early cancer. If the colonoscopy is negative, then you may not need to repeat the procedure for the ten years. Men should have a PSA test for prostate cancer and determine if it is rising higher or not. A rise of your PSA level even by 0.70ng is significant. You should be aware of the symptoms and make sure that a digital rectal examination is part of your yearly checkup. Symptoms of an enlarged prostate include difficulty in starting your urine, a narrow stream, and waking to go to the bathroom several times at night. A rectal examination is easily performed by your doctor. If the examination shows the surface of the prostate to be irregular, further evaluation is necessary to make sure it is not cancerous. Doing an ultrasound will reveal if the prostate is enlarged, but a biopsy of the nodule is the final determinant to see if there is cancer.

For determining the status of your heart, you should have an EKG, and if abnormal, further studies must be done such as a stress test or even a coronary arterial evaluation, either by an arteriogram or a CAT scan. If ever you have chest pains, you should immediately see your health provider to make sure it is not a heart attack. Also, you should have a yearly checkup of your cholesterol (LDL and HDL), triglycerides, CRP, homocysteine level, and LPA. Ask your doctor how to reduce these risks factors and make sure you know whether or not the results are getting higher. There are many good supplements that may reduce your high cholesterol and triglycerides, and at the same time increase the good cholesterol (HDL). Homocysteine is one of the substances that cause hardening of the arteries. You can prevent the rise of this substance by taking B6, folic acid, and BI2.

If you are a woman, you need to have a yearly PAP smear and conduct monthly self-breast examination to detect any mass, which, if present, must be followed with mammogram or biopsy.

As you age, if you begin to have lapses of memory (mild cognitive impairment), you should be evaluated for dementia by a competent neurologist. There are now early diagnostic procedures that will help the doctor make an early diagnosis by using a CAT scan, MRI, or PET scan following an injection of a special dye that will color the beta amyloid plaques as well as the neurofibrillary tangles in the brain. These amyloid plaques and neurofibrillary tangles are the findings of Alzheimer's disease. Likewise, a significant atrophy of the hippocampus and an increased level of beta amyloid protein precursor in the cerebrospinal fluid, plus the results of the psychoanalysis or mental function, are all important clues. Of course, your doctor has to rule out dementia rather than Alzheimer's disease. There are now good supplements available that may prevent or reverse cognitive impairment.

Having said all these things, a complete yearly checkup must include complete blood count, electrolytes, liver, kidney', thyroid, prostate, and hormonal assessments. You need also to see your dentist, your ophthalmologist, and have your hearing evaluated as well. In addition, you need to have your vaccination history, whether you need a booster or not.

Your health provider knows all the types of vaccines needed for all ages. You also need to have a chest x-ray', especially if you have a chronic cough, shortness of breath, or if you are a smoker. Finally, you need to have a bone density test to check for osteoporosis that may lead to multiple fractures of the vertebra or other bones. You also need to have Doppler studies on your carotid arteries to make sure you are not at risk to have a stroke. The presence of plaque in your arteries or in your legs may indicate hardening of your arteries elsewhere.

How about hobbies? Do you read your Bible? Do you have a strong faith in God? Do you believe in resurrection after death? Do you believe in eternal life or heaven? These questions are paramount in our life. We should assess and reassess our relationship to God. After all, God is the source and the provider of good health, wisdom, and success. Everything that is grown on earth, the fertile soil, the sun, the air, and the rain are the very source of the things that we need. Without these things, nothing can survive.

You should realize that members of the human race are basically sinners, because no one is perfect. Therefore, we should repent, apologize with contrition, and make corrections or amendments to our attitudes. We should continue to read, to search the laws of God and all the things that He wants us to do; be obedient and commit ourselves to keep and obey His commandments because that is the proof that we love God (St. John 14:14 also Proverbs 14:13). Read my article on "The Credo of a Good Christian" elsewhere in this book. This could be the most important lifestyle change that one must undertake. One should keep on searching and learning all the things that make life better and bring one closer to God, Our Creator!

Chapter 42
What Matters in Human Life

Human life has its beginning and its ends. Life's journey may be short or long; the road may be rough or smooth, or may be peaceful or turbulent. But, in general, life is enjoyable although many times it is interrupted with tears and laughter. There are those who are courageous and excel in their pursuit for financial success. Others are content in just getting by.

Indeed, people have many differences in their looks, attitudes, beliefs, habits, their gifts, and professions. No matter who you are, be honest and always speak the truth. Be yourself and never compare yourself with others or you will find yourself bitterly miserable.

- What matters in life is not how wealthy you are, but how much have you given.
- What matters in life is not how many songs you have written and sang, but the kind of songs that both inspire and make the audience shed tears of joy.
- What matters in life is not what you bought, but how much have you built.
- What matters in life is not how many good things have you learned, but how much you have taught.
- What matters in life is not how talented and competent you are, but your character.

- What matters in life is not how many people you knew but how many people feel a lasting loss when you are gone.
- What matters in life is not about your success, but your significance and the generous contributions you have given to your community.
- What matters in life is not about the mansion homes and luxurious cars you have, but your positive relationship to your family, your friends, and to your community.
- What matters in life is not just what you are doing, but doing it to the best that you can so that it may be appreciated and beneficial.
- What matters in life is not just what you think and believe, but it must be consistently noble, beautiful, inspiring, and result in tender loving care and joy.
- What matters in life is not just living to get by, but having a goal to accomplish to better yourself and others.
- What matters in life are the small good things you have discovered every day and sharing the knowledge with others to make life peaceful and enjoyable.
- Above all, what matters most in life is that you discover who you really are? Who are you?